# THE GRAIN BRAIN COOKBOOK

ALSO BY DAVID PERLMUTTER, MD

*Grain Brain*

*Power Up Your Brain*

*Raise a Smarter Child by Kindergarten*

*The Better Brain Book*

# THE
# GRAIN
# BRAIN
## COOKBOOK

*More Than 150 Life-Changing*

*Gluten-Free Recipes*

*to Transform Your Health*

## DAVID PERLMUTTER, MD

LITTLE, BROWN AND COMPANY
NEW YORK   BOSTON   LONDON

Copyright © 2014 by David Perlmutter, MD

Little, Brown and Company
Hachette Book Group
237 Park Avenue, New York, NY 10017
littlebrown.com

First Edition: September 2014

Little, Brown and Company is a division of Hachette Book Group, Inc. The Little, Brown name and logo are trademarks of Hachette Book Group, Inc.

The publisher is not responsible for websites (or their content) that are not owned by the publisher.

The Hachette Speakers Bureau provides a wide range of authors for speaking events. To find out more, go to hachettespeakersbureau.com or call (866) 376-6591.

Photographs copyright © by Stephen Pool

ISBN 978-0-316-33425-9
LCCN 2014940575

10 9 8 7 6 5 4 3 2 1

RRD-C

Printed in the United States of America

This book is dedicated to our daughter, Reisha, for helping me embrace the beauty of our world; to our son, Austin, who restores my faith in and devotion to the practice of medicine; and to my wife, Leize, whose love, understanding, and companionship have sustained and supported me on our incredible journey together.

# CONTENTS

---

# THE GRAIN BRAIN
# COOKBOOK

# INTRODUCTION

## *Welcome to a New Way of Life*

*Let food be thy medicine and medicine be thy food.*
— HIPPOCRATES, THE FATHER OF MODERN MEDICINE

SEVERAL YEARS AGO OUR beloved terrier, Teako, began losing his fur, so my wife and I decided to take him to the veterinarian. The first question the vet asked in the exam room was simply, "What are you feeding your dog?" As my wife responded, I was struck by that insightful question. Few of us are surprised when our vet asks what we are feeding our pets because we readily accept the notion that the foods they consume play a significant role in their health and wellness (and, conversely, in their risk for illness and disease). What dawned on me was how unusual it is for a doctor to similarly ask an ailing human patient, "What are you *eating*?" No doubt, most people would be taken aback by such a question, and some might even consider it offensive. They expect queries about their medications and symptoms, not inquiries about their dietary choices. Sadly, they also anticipate more drugs to add to their daily regimen, with no mention of what kinds of modifications they could be making in their eating and lifestyle habits to treat their health conditions.

Food matters. I believe that what we eat is the most important decision we make every day in terms of our health and our ability to resist and combat disease. I also believe that the shift in our diet that has occurred over the past century—from high-fat, low-carb to today's low-fat, high-carb trend, fundamentally consisting of grains and other damaging carbohydrates—is at the root of many of the modern scourges linked to the brain, including chronic headaches, insomnia, anxiety, depression, epilepsy, movement disorders, schizophrenia, attention deficit hyperactivity disorder (ADHD), and those senior moments that quite likely herald serious cognitive decline and full-blown, irreversible, untreatable, and incurable brain disease.

The idea that our brain is sensitive to what we eat has been quietly circulating in our most prestigious medical literature recently. And what cutting-edge research is finally revealing, to the bewilderment of many, is that the human brain is far more responsive to nutritional choices than we ever imagined. While it's common knowledge now that "heart smart" diets can help support the cardiovascular system, and that we can prevent osteoporosis by getting plenty of calcium and vitamin D in our diets, it's not universally appreciated yet that we can indeed affect the fate of our brain's health—for better or worse—by what we put in our mouths. Hippocrates got it right thousands of years ago when he said that food should be our medicine and medicine our food.

I covered this topic at length in my 2013 book *Grain Brain,* in which I detail how and why food impacts brain health. And I devote a lot of space in that book to explaining that we can employ the power of nutrition to prevent what's perhaps the most dreaded brain condition of all—Alzheimer's disease, an affliction for which there is no meaningful remedy whatsoever. A bold, aggressive statement to make, I know, but the science is finally here to show how this is possible. In 2013, the *New England Journal of Medicine* published the results of a new study showing that the costs for dementia care in 2010 were estimated to be as high as $200 billion, roughly twice that expended for heart disease and almost triple what was spent on cancer. By some estimates, 2.7 million Alzheimer's patients in America today might not have developed this disease, which robs its victims of their ability to respond to the world around them, if only they and their families had learned that food matters. If only my father, once a renowned neurosurgeon, had known this decades ago before his own brain plunged down the path to advanced Alzheimer's. Indeed, my mission is deeply personal. But it isn't just about ending Alzheimer's disease.

## PREVENTION IS THE CURE

I've been a practicing neurologist for the past thirty-odd years, dealing with a wide array of brain disorders and dementia on a daily basis. I work in a medical system that's unfortunately still trying to treat patients with strong drugs rather than cure them through prevention. In today's world, we're told that we can pretty much live our lives, come what may — and then, if our health is affected, we just turn to doctors to provide us with "magic pills" that (might) alleviate the problem. But you often can't take a pill to cure a brain condition. And while drugs exist to address symptoms, they won't necessarily eradicate the source of the problem. This is true whether we're talking about anxiety or migraines, depression or dementia.

One of the examples I highlight in *Grain Brain* is the incidence of ADHD in this country, which shows just how reactive rather than proactive we've become in healthcare. In the past decade, diagnosis of ADHD has increased 53 percent. I'm not convinced ADHD is a medical condition that should be treated with powerful drugs; I believe this increase is almost certainly due to what we're feeding our children. But our medical establishment too often convinces parents that the "quick fix" of medication is the best option. Indeed, 85 percent of all ADHD medications produced in the world are used exclusively in the United States, a sobering statistic. A full 11 percent of all American children now carry this diagnosis — that's 6.4 *million American children* ages four through seventeen. By definition, these metrics clearly qualify ADHD as a national epidemic. More heart wrenching is the fact that an incredible two-thirds of those children are now on medication for a problem that may have been completely preventable — and may be reversible — using diet alone. Clearly, there is something wrong with this picture.

Let me give you one more example. About 10 percent of America's adult population suffers from depression, a statistic that qualifies this condition as an epidemic as well. And while we normally don't think of depression as a "serious" illness, it's directly associated with approximately thirty thousand deaths in this country every year. Depression is almost always treated with potent pills—drugs that change the natural chemistry of the body and brain and come with many side effects. Antidepressants, in fact, are among the most prescribed drugs in America, fueling a multibillion-dollar industry.

But as I've already stated (and as I describe in detail in *Grain Brain*), depression, Alzheimer's disease, and ADHD, among other brain-related ailments, can be prevented through diet. The various medications prescribed for these conditions focus squarely on symptoms, basically treating the smoke while ignoring the fire. I argue that we need to focus on the fire itself: *inflammation*.

## YOUR #1 VILLAIN: THE SILENT KILLER

Contrary to what you might think, the inflammatory process that's involved in the degeneration in your arthritic knee or your coronary arteries is the very same one that leads to the deterioration of the human brain. Your arthritic knee is painful because it's inflamed. So what do you do? If you're like most people, you reach for an anti-inflammatory medication to put out the fire. And that's exactly what we need to do in the brain. But that doesn't mean taking a medication; it means creating an environment in which the fire never burns in the first place. That's the cornerstone of preventing every brain-related condition or disorder. As John Kennedy said, "The time to repair the roof is when the sun is shining."

Researchers have known for some time that the essence of all degenerative conditions, including brain disorders, is inflammation. But until now, scientists couldn't identify the instigators of that inflammation—the first missteps that prompt this deadly reaction. And what we are finding is that gluten (a protein found in wheat, barley, and rye) and a high-carbohydrate diet are among the most prominent stimulators of inflammatory pathways that reach the brain. What's most disturbing about this discovery is that we often don't know when our brains are being negatively affected. Digestive disorders and food allergies are much easier to spot because symptoms such as gas, bloating, pain, constipation, and diarrhea emerge relatively quickly. But the brain is a more elusive organ. It could be enduring assaults at a molecular level without your feeling it. Unless you're nursing a headache or managing an obvious neurological problem, it can be hard to know what's going on in your brain until it's too late. And once the diagnosis is in for brain disease, it's difficult to turn the train around.

Although the influence of inflammation on brain health and disease is widespread, the upside is that our food choices can directly impact inflammation. And when you consider inflammation's role in cancer, diabetes, heart disease, obesity, and virtually every other chronic condition common in Western cultures, the implications of what you eat are nothing short of life changing. I'm going to show you how to control your genetic destiny through your diet—even if you were born with a genetic tendency to develop a neurological challenge. This will require you to free yourself from two myths that many people still cling to: (1) carbs are good and (2) fat is bad.

(It's beyond the scope of this book to go into further detail about inflammation—what exactly it is, how it can become problematic in a human body, how we test for it, and so on. I examine inflammation in greater depth in *Grain Brain*, and I encourage you to go there for more information. It's a topic on which everyone should be more informed.)

## THE BLOOD SUGAR CONNECTION: WHY YOU MUST GO LOW-CARB

If you live to be eighty-five years old, and you do nothing to change your risk for brain disease today, you have a fifty-fifty chance of developing Alzheimer's disease. That's a mere flip of a coin. If you have a family history of Alzheimer's disease, your risk is dramatically increased. And if you're a type 2 diabetic, your risk is *doubled*. Now, you obviously can't change your family history, but type 2 diabetes is often an outcome of poor lifestyle choices.

The idea that your risk for Alzheimer's is tied to diabetes may seem inconceivable at first. But it makes sense when you consider the relationships shared between these two ailments. Diabetes is characterized by elevated blood sugar. And elevated blood sugar is toxic to brain cells. In a recent report in the top journal *Neurology*, researchers studied 266 healthy adults who had no cognitive difficulties. First, the researchers measured their fasting blood sugar, a test to determine how much sugar (glucose) was in their bloodstream and how well they metabolized sugar. Next, each member of the group had an MRI scan that looked at the size of the hippocampus and the amygdala, the two regions of the brain involved with cognitive function and memory. The researchers then had these same individuals come back to the laboratory four years later to repeat the MRI scans. Their findings were breathtaking: The scientists found a striking correlation between average blood sugar levels and the degree of shrinkage of these two brain parts. The higher a person's blood sugar levels, even within the "normal" range, the higher the degree of shrinkage. The scientists calculated the blood sugar to be responsible for 6 to 10 percent of the size reductions, even after factoring in other potential causes such as alcohol consumption, smoking, age, and high blood pressure.

This is empowering information, telling us that higher blood sugar levels translate directly to more aggressive brain shrinkage, specifically in the areas that determine our cognitive and memory function. And so-called normal blood sugar levels—or what we think of as normal—*are not good enough* if you want to preserve your brain and mental faculties. Make no mistake about it: your brain's health and ability to function are a direct reflection of your consumption of carbohydrates and sugars. This knowledge is what informs every recipe you're about to explore.

In August 2013, the *New England Journal of Medicine* published the results of a similar study that further confirmed the indelible link between blood sugar levels and brain health. This latest investigation documented fasting blood sugars in a group of 2,067 elderly individuals. Although some of these individuals had diabetes at the start, most did not, and none had dementia in the beginning. Over a follow-up period of almost seven years, the researchers also had participants perform mental examinations to gauge their cognitive strength. They found a nearly perfect correlation between levels of blood sugar and risk for dementia. Those with higher average blood sugar levels within the preceding five years had a statistically significant increased risk for dementia. This held true whether one started with diabetes or not.

Clearly, maintaining healthy levels of blood sugar is an important part of keeping your brain on cue as you age. The recipes throughout this book are designed to help you do just that. But we're not aiming to have just "good" blood sugar control; we're seeking excellent, total control. And the way you can achieve that control is to cut back on your carbohydrates, including plain sugar and foods that contain starches (such as breads, pastas, and potatoes). You can make healthy substitutions for all of these foods—substitutions that are just as tasty and satisfying, if not more so. I'll give you plenty of ideas about how to do this, with suggestions such as adding more nonstarchy vegetables like mixed greens and bell peppers to your plate, or trying my creative recipes that include nuts and seeds. For example, sautéed spinach with scallions and toasted pumpkin seeds (page 138) is delicious, packs in a variety of nutrients, and helps manage blood sugar.

It's not always easy to understand where sugars and carbohydrates are coming from. A 12-ounce glass of orange juice, for instance, is typically looked upon as a healthy choice. This drink has become a staple in the American diet, but it contains a whopping 36 grams of sugar. That's 9 teaspoons of sugar, about the same found in a can of cola.

At breakfast, many of us are bombarding our bodies with high levels of brain-damaging carbohydrates without even realizing it—indeed, we imagine we're starting the day in the healthiest way possible. Down your glass of orange juice and then have a bowl of whole-grain cereal with a banana or whole-wheat toast with jam…and you've just set the stage for elevated blood sugar levels that may very well lead to your brain's demise farther down the road. Like orange juice, fruit itself represents a significant source of carbohydrates in the typical American diet. To be clear, it's perfectly reasonable to have a handful of blueberries or an apple a day, but the four to six servings that are often recommended by nutrition "experts" may wreak havoc on your body's ability to process sugar.

Our goal is to keep total daily carbohydrates at or below 60 to 80 grams per day. (This certainly casts that glass of orange juice, which has about half of that daily carb load, in a new light.) If you follow the recipes in this book, you won't have to count carbs during your day. Here's what 60 to 80 grams of carbohydrates might look like: Start your day with an incredibly tasty, nutrient-packed breakfast of a Roasted Onion Omelet with Sun-Dried Tomato and Onion Chutney (page 63). For lunch, enjoy a satisfying Greek Salad (page 91) featuring fresh veggies, olives, and feta cheese with homemade vinaigrette. And how about Salmon Roasted in Butter and Almonds (page 237) for dinner, with Broccoli, Mushrooms, and Feta (page 132) on the side, and a crunchy walnut arugula salad?

If there's one thing about my diet protocol that sets it apart from others, it's that it derives a lot of flavors from fat. That's right: fat. Along with a substantial reduction in carb consumption, the very best thing you can do for your brain is to bring wonderful, healthful, life-sustaining fat back into your kitchen. Dietary fat is what we've been eating for 2.6 million years, and it's vital for the health of every cell in your body.

## A FAT DIET THAT CAN MAKE YOU SMART (AND SLENDER)

If you haven't read *Grain Brain*, you may be surprised at how much fat you'll be welcoming into your kitchen using these recipes. Dietary fat, demonized over the last several decades, is actually a super-fuel for the brain. Leading scientists now confirm that *more* fat in the diet is the way to go to ensure a healthy brain. My hope is that as you experience these delicious recipes, you'll reconnect with a love for fat, a fundamental food choice for health and longevity. And you'll learn what makes for healthful choices in the fats you reintroduce to your cooking.

Look around. Our diets have obviously changed in the past several decades, while at the same time death from brain diseases has increased dramatically. From 1979 to 2010, the number of deaths related to brain diseases in

America increased by an incredible 66 percent in men and 92 percent in women. These numbers are much higher than those in other Western countries, yet we are in no way genetically different from people in other countries. The difference lies in our food choices, and what those choices are doing to us physically.

For most of human evolution, we've eaten what we could either find or kill (until modern agriculture and manufacturing made food acquisition practically effortless). And in terms of getting enough calories to survive, fat has always been our friend. It's an optimal fuel for both the body and the brain.

Let's turn to some landmark science to prove this fact, since I realize some of you may be scratching your heads. A two-year study reported in 2008 in the *New England Journal of Medicine* followed 322 adults who were randomly placed on one of three different diets: low-fat, low-carb, or Mediterranean. (Like the low-carb diet, the Mediterranean diet emphasizes healthy fats like those from olive oil and fish, nuts and seeds, and whole fruits and vegetables, but allows for more carbs through whole grains.) The low-carb and Mediterranean diets showed the greatest weight loss, 12 pounds and 10 pounds, respectively. The researchers looked at a variety of parameters that have an important impact on health, such as weight and signs of inflammation. The study also revealed that those on the low-carb, high-fat diet had a much higher level of HDL, so-called good cholesterol, compared to the low-fat dieters. The study also examined the subjects' triglycerides, a fatty substance in blood and a huge risk factor for coronary artery disease. The people on the low-fat diet, who consumed the highest level of carbohydrates, had almost no change in their triglycerides, while the drop in triglycerides for those on the high-fat, low-carb diet was almost *ten times* greater.

But even more importantly, the study demonstrated that the presence of a biomolecule called C-reactive protein, a notable marker for inflammation, was sizably lowered only in those individuals who *ate the most fat*. Here's where the science is even more compelling. A 2012 report from the Mayo Clinic published in the *Journal of Alzheimer's Disease* showed that the risk of dementia was reduced by an astounding 44 percent in people eating a high-fat, low-carb diet compared to those who ate lower levels of fat. Those favoring the most carbs in their diets actually experienced an *increased* risk for dementia—by a whopping 89 percent.

Not all fats are created equal, however. And I'm certainly not suggesting that *being* fat is a good thing. You shouldn't be eating any trans fats or making excuses to eat a pastry every morning or cook with corn oil just because they contain fat. What you will find in prepared, low-fat, high-carbohydrate foods at the grocery store and in many of the cooking oils that sit on the shelf month after month are the highly modified fats that damage the brain (and will make you fat).

Hence, your diet should be rich in healthy sources of life-giving fat, like these:

extra-virgin olive oil
coconut oil
avocado
grass-fed beef
wild-caught (not farm-raised) fish
nuts (e.g., almonds, walnuts, pecans)
seeds (e.g., pumpkin seeds, chia seeds, sunflower seeds)

It's ideal to choose grass-fed beef, rather than grain-fed, for a few reasons. For one thing, grass-fed beef is naturally rich in brain-healthy omega-3 fats, which reduce inflammation. The meat from grain-fed cattle contains far higher levels of omega-6 fats, which actually cause inflammation. What's more, most grain-fed animals receive genetically engineered strains of feed and may well have been treated with hormones and antibiotics.

I also encourage you to eat more of nature's perfect food: eggs! These 70-calorie nutrient bombs have all of the essential amino acids we need to survive, plus vitamins, minerals, and brain-protective antioxidants. Eggs also contain cholesterol, which has been wrongly vilified for decades. Cholesterol is a fundamental component of every cell membrane in your body, and the precursor for all the steroid hormones in the body and even vitamin D. Moreover, it's associated with a more than 70 percent reduced risk of dementia in the elderly.

Cholesterol is one of the most important biochemicals for healthy brain function and, indeed, for human health in general. Cholesterol is so vital for brain health that even though the brain represents only about 2 to 3 percent of your body weight, 25 percent of the entire cholesterol content of your body is in your brain, where it performs critical roles to facilitate the brain's complex operations. It also strengthens, nourishes, and protects brain cells, and helps clear away harmful free radicals.

The current war on cholesterol, especially as it relates to cardiovascular disease and risk for heart attack, is absolutely unfounded. We desperately need cholesterol in order to be healthy. In fact, every cell in your body manufactures cholesterol because it's so essential. Research has already proven that people with the lowest levels of cholesterol have a significantly higher risk for depression, suicide, and, in the elderly, dementia and even death. Some research indicates that in folks aged eighty-five or older, higher cholesterol is associated with extraordinary *resistance* to dementia. And yet, the pharmaceutical industry would have you believe that cholesterol is your enemy and that you should do everything you can, including taking powerful drugs, to lower the amount of this pivotal chemical. In my professional opinion, it's rarely, if ever, appropriate to consider high cholesterol alone to be a significant threat to health if you're engaging in a healthy lifestyle that limits the true drivers of cardiovascular disease — smoking, excess alcohol consumption, lack of aerobic exercise, overweight, and a diet high in carbohydrates. In fact, the best lab report to refer to in determining your health status is not cholesterol levels, it's hemoglobin A1C, a snapshot of your average blood sugar level over the previous three months. The higher your A1C level, regardless of cholesterol, the higher your risk for brain disease. When you talk to your doctor about these ideas (and you absolutely should), be prepared for responses that are founded on emotions and not on current science. (See *Grain Brain* for more facts and for a comprehensive discussion of this topic.)

Since cholesterol plays such a crucial role in health, and specifically brain health, we have to revamp our notions about what constitutes a good diet. We've all been told that we shouldn't eat eggs because they are high in cholesterol and saturated fat. But in 2013, the medical journal *Metabolism* published a stunning report evaluating the results of blood tests from people who eat eggs versus egg substitutes. The researchers found that those who ate real eggs actually had *improvement* in various blood tests that measure health in terms of risk for cardiovascular disease, diabetes, and brain disorders. The truth is that we've been eating saturated fat for over two million years. And the science is now showing that saturated fat is *not* the enemy in terms of heart disease. The culprit is sugar and carbohydrates.

What matters most in terms of your diet is that you lower carbohydrates and increase healthy fats. I encourage my patients to eat lean, grass-fed beef and dairy products and pasture-raised poultry and eggs—all of which contain cholesterol. It's good for them. It's good for all of us.

## THE WHOLE-GRAIN TRUTH: WHY YOU MUST DITCH GLUTEN

As I just described, ongoing inflammation plays a major role in compromising brain health and function. And many things can trigger inflammatory processes in the body: injury and illness due to an invading germ or virus; chronic conditions like cancer, obesity, and anxiety; environmental factors like smoking, pollution, and poor sleep; or a food ingredient to which the immune system adversely reacts. One of my main messages in *Grain Brain* is about the deleterious effect that a particular protein called gluten can have on the body. As the name implies, it's like glue. Gluten is the sticky stuff that allows us to make pizza dough, bread, pasta, and pastries. But our physiology was never designed to deal with this relatively new and very strange protein. When our bodies encounter something foreign and unusual, we typically mount an immune response. And that means inflammation.

Over the past decade researchers around the world have begun to discover that being sensitive to gluten can substantially increase inflammation throughout the human body. This is frightening because gluten is in a lot of the food we're eating today—anything made with wheat, barley, or rye. And what makes it even worse is that gluten is frequently found in the very foods we're told are "healthy," such as whole grains. Every day we read claims on food packaging and in advertising about "whole-grain goodness." At the same time, we hear about the benefits of low-fat this or that, and we conclude that we should be avoiding fat and embracing whole grains.

I'm going to assume that you're already somewhat familiar with gluten and the trend in going gluten-free, as it's made a lot of headlines in the past couple of years. (Again, for an in-depth exploration of this topic, see *Grain Brain*.) The reason it's receiving so much attention now is that the science is very compelling, especially as it relates to brain health. To clarify, I'm not just talking about celiac disease, a rare autoimmune disorder whereby individuals have a unique sensitivity to gluten that involves the small intestine. I'm talking about a type of gluten sensitivity that may affect up to 30 percent of us, one that has been linked to a variety of neurological problems beyond dementia, including movement disorders, epilepsy, and muscle disorders. It has also been linked to conditions such as ADHD, depression, headaches, migraines, damage to the nerves (called neuropathy), and even schizophrenia.

As soon as the neurological community began to recognize inflammation as the root cause of a vast array of brain conditions, I began testing virtually every one of my patients for gluten sensitivity whether they were complaining of headaches or memory lapses.

The results were eye opening, as I witnessed my patients improve from long-standing conditions just by going gluten-free. People who'd been plagued by chronic neurological disorders from crushing migraines and epilepsy to relentless anxiety and depression were suddenly freed from their conditions. So I began to evangelize to anyone who would listen—patients and colleagues alike—about the importance not only of a low-carbohydrate diet, but also of screening for gluten sensitivity and getting people who are gluten sensitive on a gluten-free diet. These are the most powerful interventions I have learned in my thirty years of practicing medicine.

At this point, I know what you're wondering: Haven't we always consumed wheat, and therefore gluten? Our consumption of wheat actually began about ten thousand years ago, with the advent of agriculture. That might seem like a long time to many people. In reality, though, for more than 99 percent of our time on this planet we've been essentially wheat- and gluten-free.

And why is this important? Our genes are pretty much exactly the same as they have been for at least the past fifty thousand years, and these are the genes that dictate which foods we can tolerate. Genetically, we are not prepared to eat wheat—an ingredient that now makes up 20 percent of all calories that we as humans consume. With devastating consequences.

To many, bashing wheat and gluten is almost sacrilegious. We're told, "Give us this day our daily bread." And whether it's matzo, the unleavened bread eaten at the Jewish holiday of Passover, or the wafers representing the body of Christ given at communion, you can see why some people may consider this blasphemy. And what about the expression "the greatest thing since sliced bread"? Truth be told, brain disease starts with your daily bread.

The wheat consumed in biblical times is not representative of what passes for wheat today, which is subject to aggressive hybridization. Today's wheat renders a product that our physiology cannot process. And as you know by now, when you challenge your body with foods that it cannot recognize, you're creating the perfect environment to increase inflammation.

It's essential to understand that our food is more than just the macronutrients of fat, protein, and carbohydrates, or the micronutrients like minerals and vitamins. Food is information, and it plays an important role in controlling our DNA. It's true: the expression of your genes is dictated by the foods you choose to eat.

We can eat foods that "turn on" certain genes, genes that then make chemicals that increase inflammation. Or we can choose to eat foods that fundamentally reduce inflammation and increase our body's genetically programmed production of antioxidants that protect us from the ravaging effects of inflammation. You can control your genetic destiny through diet and lifestyle—it's as simple as that. The key thing to remember is that the ultimate goal is to control inflammation. And this is achieved through my dietary protocol, which has the power to reduce inflammation directly and indirectly by supporting a healthy expression of genes related to longevity and anti-inflammatory pathways.

## THE GRAIN BRAIN DIET

Last year an eighty-year-old woman was brought into my office by her two sons because she was failing mentally. She hadn't yet been formally diagnosed with Alzheimer's, but she was unable to follow a conversation and was even beginning to have problems with everyday tasks such as dressing and preparing meals. She had been to a brain specialist who prescribed a medicine that, according to her sons, had only made things worse (unfortunately, a common occurrence). We ultimately found that she was sensitive to gluten but had no intestinal distress or celiac disease. At that point I put her on a gluten-free, low-carbohydrate, higher-fat diet. Within a few weeks, one of her sons described her transformation bluntly: "It's as if she's awakened, and we have our mom back." This is treating the fire, the cause of a problem, not just the smoke. And this is my wish for you on this diet. Even if you're not currently harboring a fire within, this diet will have a profound impact on how your body's computer—your brain—will be working next year, in five years, and, really, for the rest of your life.

I realize how hard it is for many people to give up their beloved bread, pasta, and desserts, but what follows are recipes that will give you the keys to the kingdom: delicious, low-carb, high-fat, and gluten-free meal plans. I suggest that you follow the four-week program that I outline in *Grain Brain*, which will help you ease into this new lifestyle. Of course, it's good practice to check with your physician before beginning any new diet regimen, particularly if you have existing health issues, such as diabetes or heart disease.

Once you begin to follow my dietary guidelines and use the recipes in this book, you will achieve some pretty important goals relatively quickly. You'll shift your body away from relying on carbohydrates for fuel, cut cravings for sugar, feel energized (and hopefully gravitate to more exercise), move into a restful sleep pattern, and establish a new rhythm for long-term, healthy living.

Making dietary changes, even small ones, can seem overwhelming at first. You wonder how you can avoid your usual habits and favorite foods. Will you feel deprived and hungry? Will you find it impossible to keep up this new lifestyle forever? I can hear you already: *How can I go without a slice of pizza? How can I ever eat in a restaurant? How do I celebrate with family and friends? But life without sweets is not possible!*

Believe me, I've heard it all. My answer to these laments is very straightforward. This is not punishment; it is the path to great health and enjoyment. The sooner you experience the rewards of this diet, the sooner you'll never think about pizza and pastries again (nor crave them). Just like everyone else, I go to parties, attend conferences, and celebrate events that put me face to face with the enemy. But I never find myself negotiating whether to eat that pie or reach for the breadbasket. The thought never crosses my mind. And it won't for you either once you take the initial plunge and feel the effects.

Many of us eat out several times a week, especially while we're at work, so it's imperative that we learn how to navigate restaurant menus while sticking with this protocol. It's actually easier than you'd initially think. The guidelines in this cookbook will allow you to make healthful food choices when dining out or traveling. Although the meat may not be grass-fed or the chicken pasture-raised, and the vegetables may not be organic, there is usually plenty to eat that is low-carb and free of gluten, and you can easily pass on those foods that are not. It's not that hard to make any menu work for you as long as you're savvy about your decisions. Restaurants usually offer meats and fish that can be cooked to your liking, and nowadays the side dishes are often ordered separately. Baked fish with steamed vegetables is likely to be a safe bet (hold the potatoes and breadbasket, and ask for a side salad with olive oil and vinegar). Watch out for elaborate dishes that contain multiple ingredients. And when in doubt, ask your server or the chef about the dishes. Once you get used to using the recipes in this book, you'll find it much easier to know what to order when you're out, as well as what to request in terms of substitutes so you can stay on track.

You'd be surprised by what a little experimentation in the kitchen can do to turn a classic dish filled with gluten and inflammatory ingredients into an equally delicious but brain-friendly meal. Instead of regular flour or wheat, you'll use coconut flour, nut meals like ground almonds, and ground flaxseed; in lieu of sugar, you'll sweeten your recipes with stevia or small amounts of whole fruits (until you're ready to fully disconnect yourself from sweets); and rather than cook with processed vegetable oils, you'll stick with old-fashioned butter and extra-virgin olive oil.

And when you're faced with temptation (the box of doughnuts at work or a friend's birthday cake), remind yourself that you'll pay for the indulgence. Be willing to accept those consequences if you cannot say no. A grain brain–free way of life is, in my humble opinion, the most fulfilling and gratifying way of life there is. Enjoy it.

As you'll soon discover, I've gathered a terrific selection of recipes that will make your move into a healthier way of life absolutely stress-free in the kitchen. These meals are easy to prepare, fun to serve, and downright delicious to eat. The additional bonus is that as you spend time in your own kitchen cooking these wonderful dishes, you will see the weight fall off and, should you choose to have them, laboratory tests will show vast improvements in many areas of your biochemistry. Perhaps most importantly, if your brain could talk out loud, you would hear it say that it is happy and functioning at its highest level. Aren't those good enough reasons to say good-bye to gluten and most carbohydrates, and say hello to healthy fat?

# THE *GRAIN BRAIN* PANTRY

---

IF YOU'RE FAMILIAR WITH my book *Grain Brain*, you know what lies ahead. No more bread, pasta, pastry, soy, or sugars. Even most products labeled "gluten-free" or "sugar-free" are banished. But don't panic: that's where this cookbook is here to help. I'm going to show you how you can conquer your cravings for sugar, wheat, and addictive carbs while still eating with enormous satisfaction and achieving optimal health. You'll quickly discover that it is worth the effort as you spend your days with clearer thoughts, better sleep, and renewed energy.

As you begin your new way of life in the kitchen, I suggest that you learn to grocery shop when you are *not* hungry, and with a shopping list in hand. This prevents spur-of-the-moment purchases, which usually fall into the not-good-for-you category. You'll find that most healthy foods (fresh produce, meats, and dairy products) are located around the perimeter of the grocery store, while the "bad guys" (prepackaged, processed foods) are usually in the middle aisles, so steer clear of those toxic areas. "Health food" stores are often just as much at fault in terms of the prepared foods and packaged foods that they offer. To me, your best bet is your local farmers' market, where you are almost always assured that the vegetables are grown free of pesticides and other potentially harmful growth aids, and the meat, poultry, and fish come as nature intended. Of course, I do understand that shopping in this way can be expensive, but I think spending a little extra money to splurge on brain-friendly nutrition is worth it. The old adage "pay me now or pay me later" is extremely relevant here, for if you don't spend money on good nutrition today, you'll be spending money on expensive treatments later for ailments that you could have avoided altogether.

All of the recipes in this book were tested using organic produce, pasture-raised or grass-fed poultry and meats, wild-caught fish and shellfish, and farm-fresh eggs. Unsalted butter, extra-virgin olive oil, coconut oil, unsweetened nut milks, and unadulterated herbs and spices are also part and parcel of putting the recipes together. It is important that you use the same high-quality ingredients when cooking on your own. If you don't have a local farmers' market, you will find that many of these high-quality products are available at large supermarkets, chain stores, and specialty food shops, as well as online.

The eggs (remember, these are nature's perfect food) used in all of these recipes were direct-from-the-farm, but I realize that this is not always possible. You should, however, be aware of the different terminology used in commercial egg distribution, since eggs are so important in this diet. Following is a little tutorial so you will know which eggs to buy.

- **Organic eggs** designate the feed and land on which the hens were raised rather than how they were raised. The hens may be held in cages or in open space but, in most instances, they are cage-free. USDA organic certification requires that the feed used must have been produced on land that has had no toxins, chemical fertilizers, or pesticides applied for a minimum of three years. The hens cannot receive any antibiotics, hormones, invasive drugs, growth aids, or vaccines and must be given only organic, non–genetically engineered feed.

- **Free-range eggs** are those gathered from hens that have indoor quarters but are allowed free roam in the outdoors (though often in an enclosed or fenced area). There is no stipulation about feed or drug use in their maintenance.

- **Cage-free eggs** simply imply that the hens are not raised in cages, but in some type of floor arrangement with nest crates in which they can lay their eggs. Again, there is no stipulation about feed or drug use in their maintenance.

But before you stock your pantry with all of these good foods, you'll have to sweep your kitchen clean of any items not allowed on this diet. The following list is long, so get some big boxes and pack up all of these banned foods and food products:

## Avoid these grains and starches:

Barley, bulgur, couscous, farina, graham flour, Kamut, matzo meal, rye, semolina, spelt, triticale, wheat, wheat germ

All foods containing these grains and starches, including baked goods, bread, breaded food items, breadcrumbs, cakes, cereals, cookies, crackers, doughnuts, muffins, pasta, pastries, pretzels

## Avoid these general foods:

Agave, canned baked beans, beer, blue cheeses, candy, chips, commercially prepared chocolate milk, chutneys, cold cuts, communion wafers, cooking oils (soybean, corn, cottonseed, canola, peanut, safflower, grape seed, sunflower, rice bran), corn products, dried fruits, egg substitutes, energy bars, flavored coffees and teas, frozen yogurt, fruit fillings, gravies, honey, hot dogs, ice cream, instant hot drinks, jams (and jellies and preserves), juices, ketchup, malt vinegar, maple syrup, margarine, marinades, commercially prepared mayonnaise, non-dairy creamer, oats and oat bran (unless certified gluten-free), pizza, potatoes, processed cheeses (such as Velveeta) and cheese spreads, puddings, roasted nuts, salad dressings, sausages, seitan, sherbets, sodas, commercially prepared soups (and bouillons and broths), soy sauce, sports/energy drinks, sugar (all types), sweet potatoes/yams, teriyaki sauce, trail mix, vegetable shortening, vodka, wheatgrass, wine coolers

■ **Avoid** all packaged foods labeled "fat-free" or "low-fat" unless they are authentically "fat-free" or "low-fat," such as vinegars, mustards, water, etc.

■ **Avoid** all unfermented soy products (such as tofu, bean curd, and soy milk) and processed foods made with soy. Always check for "soy protein isolate" in the list of ingredients in any processed food. Eliminate all soy burgers, soy cheese, soy hot dogs, soy nuggets, soy ice cream, and soy milk yogurt. Although some naturally brewed soy sauces are technically gluten-free, many commercial brands have trace amounts of gluten.

■ **Avoid packaged products that contain these ingredients, which are "code words" for gluten:** Amino peptide complex, *Avena sativa*, brown rice syrup, caramel color (frequently made from barley), cyclodextrin, dextrin, fermented grain extract, *Hordeum distichon*, *Hordeum vulgare*, hydrolysate, hydrolyzed malt extract, hydrolyzed vegetable protein, maltodextrin, modified food starch, natural flavoring, phytosphingosine extract, *Secale cereale*, soy protein, *Triticum aestivum*, *Triticum vulgare*, hydrolized vegetable protein (HVP), yeast extract.

Now that your kitchen is low-carb and gluten-free, you can restock with products that will make cooking a brain-healthy diet a cinch. When shopping, take care when eyeing those products labeled and marketed as "gluten-free," "low-carb," "sugar-free," and all of the other health claims. Some of these foods might be just fine if they did not contain gluten or a high dosage of carbohydrates to begin with. But generally these labels come about because the foods have been highly processed, and one unhealthy ingredient has been replaced with another that is equally worrisome. In addition, by law, trace amounts of gluten or sugars may remain in processed items even if the label says they are free of them. And although the FDA issued a regulation in August 2013 to define the term "gluten-free" (and variations like "free of gluten" and "no gluten") for food labeling, it still leaves the burden on the manufacturers to comply and be accountable for using the claim truthfully. All of this confirms what I have already been saying: You're better off preparing your own food than relying on packaged products sold at the grocery store. And when you do have to buy packaged products, you must be extremely well informed and prepared to carefully read the labels of all packaged items.

Now you are ready to shop.

The following items can be consumed liberally when you're ridding yourself of grain brain. The preference is always fresh, local, and organic, but individually quick frozen (IQF) organic foods can also be used. IQF foods have been flash-frozen in individual pieces, such as a single shrimp or blueberry, thereby preventing the frozen items from massing together and forming a solid block of icy food; they should ideally be organically grown as well.

### Healthy oils and fats

Almond butter
Avocado oil
Cashew butter
Coconut oil
Extra-virgin olive oil
Ghee
Organic or pasture-fed butter
Tahini
Walnut oil

### Raw or cured fruit fats

Avocados
Coconuts
Olives

### Nut milks

Unsweetened almond milk
Unsweetened coconut milk

### Nuts

All raw or toasted nuts, except peanuts, which are a legume (Note: When buying commercially packaged roasted nuts, check the label, as they might have been processed with sugars or oils that should be avoided.)

### Dairy products

All cheeses except blue or highly processed cheeses (such as Velveeta or American slices)

## Seeds

Chia seeds
Flaxseed
Pumpkin seeds
Sesame seeds
Sunflower seeds

## Herbs, seasonings, and condiments

All fresh and dried herbs, spices, and rhizomes

Many commercially packed condiments and seasonings, such as mustards, horseradish, salsas, tapenades, vinegars, and herb/spice mixtures can be used if they were made without the addition of wheat-derived vinegars or any sweetener other than natural stevia. Be aware that some packaged products are made at plants that process wheat and/or soy and thus may be contaminated.

## Vegetables

Alfalfa sprouts
Artichokes
Asparagus
Beets
Bell peppers
Bok choy
Broccoli
Broccoli rabe
Brussels sprouts
Cabbage
Cauliflower
Celery
Collards
Cucumbers
Eggplants
Fennel
Garlic
Green beans
Haricots verts
Jicama
Kale
Kohlrabi
Leafy lettuces and greens
Leeks
Mushrooms
Mustard greens
Onions
Plantains
Pumpkins
Radishes

Rutabaga

Sauerkraut

Scallions

Shallots

Spinach

Summer squashes and squash
    blossoms

Swiss chard

Tomatillos

Turnips

Water chestnuts

Watercress

Winter squashes

Yellow wax beans

*Low-sugar fruits* (Note: Those with an asterisk [*] are substantially higher in sugar, so consume these in moderation. There's nothing wrong with adding a fresh grapefruit to your breakfast, but you wouldn't want to then eat peaches and pears or other high-sugar fruits later that day.)

Avocados

Grapefruits*

Kiwis*

Lemons

Limes

Nectarines*

Orange zest

Peaches*

Pears*

Plums*

Tomatoes

Commercially packed pickles if
    no wheat-derived vinegar or
    sweeteners are used — check
    the label

*Proteins*

Whole eggs

Wild fish

    Black cod

    Halibut

    Herring

    Grouper

    Mahimahi

    Red snapper

    Salmon

Sardines

Sea bass

Trout

Shellfish and mollusks

    Calamari (squid)

    Clams

    Crab

    Lobster

    Mussels

Octopus
Oysters
Shrimp
Grass-fed or pasture-raised meats
    Beef
    Bison/buffalo
    Lamb
    Pork
    Veal
Grass-fed organ meats
    Brain
    Heart
    Liver

Kidneys
Sweetbreads
Tongue
Free-range, organic poultry and
    wild birds
    Chicken
    Duck
    Goose
    Guinea fowl
    Ostrich
    Quail
    Turkey

**The following foods can be used in moderation.** Moderation means that you may eat small amounts (no more than 1 serving) of these ingredients once a day. Again, if you follow the recipes in this book, you'll learn how to smartly consume these ingredients. I don't intend for you to have to count carbs or weigh your food. The general principles outlined in this book will teach you how to make this new way of life effortless.

*Nongluten grains*

Amaranth
Buckwheat
Millet
Oats (Note: Although oats do not naturally contain gluten, if they are processed at mills that also handle wheat, they are frequently contaminated. Avoid oats unless they come with a guarantee that they are gluten-free.)
Quinoa
Rice (brown, white, wild)
Sorghum
Teff

Nongluten flours used in very small amounts for dusting, coating, or
    thickening sauces only:
Tapioca starch
Chestnut flour
Brown rice flour

## *Legumes*

Dried beans
Lentils
Dried peas

## *Vegetables*

Carrots
Parsnips

## *Full-fat dairy products* (Use very sparingly in recipes or as a topping.)

Cottage cheese
Cream
Kefir
Milk
Yogurt

## *Whole sweet fruits* (Note: Those with an asterisk [*] are substantially higher in sugar, so consume these only as a special treat, and then only in moderation.)

Apples
Apricots*
Bananas
Berries (best choice)
Cherries
Grapes
Mangos*
Melons*

Papayas*
Pineapples*
Pomegranates

## Sweeteners

Natural stevia
Dark chocolate having at least 70 percent cacao content

## Flavorings

Unsweetened dark cocoa powder

## Alcohol

Wine, preferably red, but no more than one glass a day

# BASICS

———

HERE ARE A FEW recipes that will help you create terrific meals that fit into the grain brain–free regimen. The most important ones are homemade stocks (both chicken and beef) and mayonnaise, simply because they are used so often. A superb homemade stock pulled from the freezer can quickly turn into a satisfying lunch with the addition of some chopped greens and/or other vegetables, or a dinner with meat or cheese added. The sauces are clever multitaskers that can add zest to egg, vegetable, and meat dishes. I've included recipes for my favorite vinaigrettes, too, as well as a spice mix for adding zing to grilled meats.

# Basic Stock

Stocks are fundamental kitchen staples, and a homemade stock is even more essential when you're freeing yourself from grain brain, because many commercially prepared stocks or broths are laden with unnecessary ingredients and can be high in salt. When you make stock yourself, you have control over the ingredients, the seasoning, and the outcome.

For a rich stock, roast the bones first; if you want a really rich stock, add pieces of fresh meat to the roasting bones. Bones that are not roasted will result in a stock that is lighter in both color and flavor.

Be sure to use cold water when making stock. This ensures that the collagen (the gelatin-forming agent) is extracted from the bones as the liquid heats. Adding the bones to hot water would seal them, keeping the collagen inside, and since much of the flavor comes from the collagen and cartilage, you don't want to lose any of the deliciousness.

If you don't want to make stock, buy the best quality canned or boxed low-sodium organic chicken or beef broth you can find, and keep a supply in the pantry for last-minute kitchen emergencies.

---

4 pounds chicken, beef, or veal bones (raw, leftover, or roasted)

1 carrot, peeled and chopped

1 celery rib, chopped

1 small onion, chopped

6 peppercorns

5 flat-leaf parsley sprigs

2 bay leaves

---

Place the bones in a large stockpot and cover with cold water by at least 2 inches. (Do not add salt to the water; salt can be added when you use the stock in a recipe.) Bring to a boil over medium-high heat.

Add the carrot, celery, onion, peppercorns, parsley, and bay leaves. Be sure to skim off the scum that rises to the top. Again, bring to a boil; then, lower the heat to a bare simmer and cook, skimming frequently, until the stock is very flavorful, about 1 hour.

Remove the pot from the heat and pour the contents through a fine-mesh strainer into a clean container. If you want a very clear stock, put a double layer of cheesecloth in the strainer before pouring.

Place the container of strained stock in a large bowl of ice to chill quickly. As it chills, the fat will rise to the top (along with any impurities); skim off and discard it.

When cool, pour the stock into small (perhaps 1-cup) containers for ease of use, cover, and store in the refrigerator for up to 2 days or in the freezer for up to 3 months.

*Chicken Stock: Nutritional Analysis per Serving (1 cup): calories 10, carbohydrates 1 g, fiber 0 g, protein 2 g, fat 0 g, sodium 65 mg, sugar 0 g*
*Beef Stock: Nutritional Analysis per Serving (1 cup): calories 15, carbohydrates 1 g, fiber 3 g, protein 4 g, fat 0 g, sodium 75 mg, sugar 1 g*

# Basic Vinaigrette

This vinaigrette keeps well, covered and refrigerated. Not only is it a quick salad dressing, but it also adds flavor when drizzled on grilled fish, shellfish, pork, or poultry.

1½ cups extra-virgin olive oil

6 tablespoons red or white wine vinegar

Salt and pepper

Combine the oil and vinegar in a resealable container — a glass jar with a lid works well. Season with salt and pepper to taste, cover, and shake vigorously to emulsify.

Use immediately, or cover and store at room temperature for up to 3 days or in the refrigerator for up to 1 month. If refrigerated, bring to room temperature and shake to blend before using.

**VARIATIONS:** You can add 1 small minced shallot and/or 1 tablespoon minced fresh flat-leaf parsley or chives to the basic recipe.

*Nutritional Analysis per Serving (1 tablespoon): calories 90, carbohydrates 0 g, fiber 0 g, protein 0 g, fat 11 g, sodium 37 mg, sugar 0 g*

# Balsamic Vinaigrette

MAKES ABOUT 2 CUPS

This is one of the most useful vinaigrettes to have as a pantry staple. It is a perfect drizzle for grilled vegetables, meats, poultry, or meaty fish, as well as a delicious salad topper.

---

1½ cups extra-virgin olive oil

½ cup balsamic vinegar

1 teaspoon Dijon mustard

Salt and pepper

---

Combine the oil, vinegar, and mustard in a resealable container—a glass jar with a lid works well. Season with salt and pepper to taste, cover, and shake vigorously to emulsify.

Use immediately, or cover and store at room temperature for up to 3 days or in the refrigerator for up to 1 month. If refrigerated, bring to room temperature and shake to blend before using.

**VARIATIONS:** You can add 1 small minced shallot and/or 1 tablespoon minced fresh basil, flat-leaf parsley, or chives to the basic recipe.

*Nutritional Analysis per Serving (1 tablespoon): calories 92, carbohydrates 1 g, fiber 0 g, protein 0 g, fat 11 g, sodium 41 mg, sugar 18 g*

# Italian Vinaigrette

MAKES ABOUT 1½ CUPS

If you use fresh herbs for this dressing, it won't be traditionally Italian because true Italian cooks prefer dried. Fresh herbs also offer an entirely different flavor than dried. The ratio of oil to vinegar here is different than in a classic French vinaigrette and makes the mixture quite acidic. This recipe works best on salads with firm lettuces or those that predominantly feature vegetables. It also makes a wonderful marinade for steaks or chops.

½ cup red wine vinegar

1 teaspoon minced garlic

1 teaspoon dried oregano

1 teaspoon dried parsley

1 cup extra-virgin olive oil

Salt and pepper

Combine the vinegar, garlic, oregano, and parsley in a resealable container—a glass jar with a lid works well. Add the olive oil, season with salt and pepper to taste, cover, and shake vigorously to emulsify.

Use immediately, or cover and store at room temperature for up to 3 days or in the refrigerator for up to 1 week. If refrigerated, bring to room temperature and shake to blend before using.

*Nutritional Analysis per Serving (1 tablespoon): calories 121, carbohydrates 0 g, fiber 0 g, protein 0 g, fat 14 g, sodium 75 mg, sugar 0 g*

# Spiced Vinaigrette

The toasted spice in this vinaigrette makes it a wonderful drizzle for grilled meats or fish as well as an aromatic dressing for vegetable salads. Although it calls for toasted cumin, you can use curry powder, Aleppo pepper, or any savory spice you like (avoid sweet spices like cinnamon). If you are using seeds, it is always best to toast them and then grind them into a powder in a spice grinder. However, even preground spices and spice mixes are enhanced by toasting.

---

1 cup extra-virgin olive oil

⅓ cup freshly squeezed lemon juice

2 tablespoons freshly ground toasted cumin

Salt and pepper

---

Combine the oil, lemon juice, and cumin in a resealable container—a glass jar with a lid works well. Season with salt and pepper to taste, cover, and shake vigorously to emulsify.

Use immediately, or cover and store at room temperature for up to 3 days or in the refrigerator for up to 1 week. If refrigerated, bring to room temperature and shake to blend before using.

*Nutritional Analysis per Serving (1 tablespoon): calories 93, carbohydrates 1 g, fiber 0 g, protein 0 g, fat 11 g, sodium 55 mg, sugar 0 g*

# Tomato Sauce

This basic tomato sauce can be used as a component of casseroles or gratins or as the base for a more flavorful sauce when herbs, spices, vegetables, and/or meats are added. Of course, in the height of summer when tomatoes are at their most delicious, by all means make this sauce with fresh-off-the-vine ones.

2 (28-ounce) cans chopped plum tomatoes, with their juice

1 cup canned tomato puree

¼ cup unsalted butter

Salt and pepper

Combine the tomatoes and the puree in a heavy-bottomed saucepan over low heat. When hot, begin adding the butter in small amounts until it blends into the sauce. Season with salt and pepper to taste and continue to cook until the sauce has thickened slightly. It is hard to give an exact time as it will depend upon the liquid in the tomatoes and the looseness of the puree, but it should be no more than 30 minutes.

Use immediately, or remove from the heat and set aside to cool. Cover and store in the refrigerator for up to 1 week or in the freezer for up to 3 months. If freezing, it is a good idea to do so in 1-cup containers for ease of use.

*Nutritional Analysis per Serving (½ cup): calories 65, carbohydrates 7 g, fiber 2 g, protein 2 g, fat 4 g, sodium 283 mg, sugar 5 g*

# Mayonnaise

Although jarred mayonnaise is in almost everybody's refrigerator, it is so simple to make and tastes so good that I recommend you make your own. This gives you the assurance that it is both gluten- and carbohydrate-free. You can make mayonnaise by hand using a whisk, but the blender method is quicker and easier on your wrist.

3 large egg yolks, at room temperature (see Note)

½ teaspoon salt

¼ teaspoon dry mustard

1 tablespoon champagne vinegar or freshly squeezed lemon juice

1½ to 2 cups extra-virgin olive oil or avocado oil

Fill the blender jar with boiling water and set it aside for a couple of minutes. (You need to heat the jar to help the eggs thicken.) Pour out the water and quickly wipe the jar dry.

Place the jar on the motor. Add the egg yolks and process on medium until very thick. Add the salt and mustard and quickly incorporate. Add the vinegar and process to blend.

With the motor running, begin pouring in the oil through the hole in the lid at an excruciatingly slow drip. The slower the drip, the more even the emulsification. When about half of the oil has been added, you should have a sauce that is like old-fashioned heavy cream, and you can begin adding the oil just a bit more quickly, as curdling will no longer be an issue. Continue adding the oil until the mayonnaise has a soft, creamy consistency. If it seems too thick after you have added all of the oil, add just a smidge more vinegar or just enough hot water to smooth the mix.

Scrape the mayonnaise into a clean container with a lid. Cover and store in the refrigerator for up to 5 days.

**VARIATIONS:** To the above recipe, you can add minced fresh herbs, minced seeded green or red hot chiles or bell peppers, grated ginger root, or grated fresh horseradish to taste. Ground spices can also vary the flavor; cumin, cayenne, and cracked black pepper are favorite additions.

**NOTE:** Although we have all heard concerns about eating uncooked eggs, if you use high-quality eggs that have been properly stored, along with the quantity of acid called for in this recipe, there should be no risk. However, homemade mayonnaise does not keep, even covered and refrigerated, for long periods of time. It is best consumed when made.

*Nutritional Analysis per Serving (1 tablespoon): calories 95, carbohydrates 0 g, fiber 0 g, protein 0 g, fat 11 g, sodium 37 mg, sugar 0 g*

# Easy Hollandaise Sauce

MAKES ABOUT ¾ CUP

Blender hollandaise was introduced, I believe, by Julia Child in the late 1960s. It made home cooks much more willing to try recipes calling for hollandaise, as the classic method takes skill and patience. Although best known as the sauce for eggs Benedict (page 60), it can also turn a dish of steamed vegetables into an elegant and satisfying meal.

3 large egg yolks, at room temperature

1 tablespoon freshly squeezed lemon juice, strained

¾ teaspoon salt, or to taste

½ teaspoon Tabasco sauce, or to taste

½ cup clarified butter (see Note), melted

Bring a few inches of water to a boil in the bottom half of a double boiler set over high heat.

Place the egg yolks, lemon juice, salt, and Tabasco in a blender and process on medium speed for 45 seconds. With the blender running, add the hot clarified butter through the hole in the lid in a very slow, steady stream and process until the mixture is very smooth and slightly thickened.

Scrape the sauce from the blender into the top half of the double boiler and set it on the bottom half to keep warm until ready to use.

NOTE: Clarified butter is the clear liquid that appears when the butterfat separates from the water and milk solids in slowly melted butter. To make clarified butter, cut 1 pound of unsalted butter into cubes and place it in a medium saucepan over very low heat. Cook, without stirring and without allowing the butter to bubble or brown, for 20 minutes. Strain the yellow liquid that rises to the top into a clean container, discarding all of the solids at the bottom. Cool to room temperature; then, cover and store in the refrigerator for up to 1 week or in the freezer for up to 6 months. Reheat the clarified butter as needed. Some grocery stores sell Indian-style clarified butter, called ghee. Ghee is made in much the same way as plain clarified butter, but it is allowed to brown a bit to caramelize the milk solids, and it often has added spices or herbs.

*Nutritional Analysis per Serving (3 tablespoons): calories 294, carbohydrates 1 g, fiber 0 g, protein 2 g, fat 31 g, sodium 445 mg, sugar 0 g*

# Chimichurri

This is my version of the classic Argentinean meat condiment. Although especially wonderful on steaks, it can be used on almost anything, from seafood to meat to vegetables, to add a delightfully fresh flavor. It should be made no more than a couple of hours before using so that the herbs retain their bright color and taste. It is one of the most refreshing sauces I know.

---

2 cups chopped fresh flat-leaf parsley

½ cup chopped scallions, green and white parts

2 tablespoons chopped fresh oregano

2 tablespoons chopped fresh cilantro

1 tablespoon minced garlic

Juice and grated zest of 1 lemon

1 cup extra-virgin olive oil

3 tablespoons white wine vinegar

Salt and pepper

---

Combine the parsley, scallions, oregano, cilantro, garlic, lemon juice, and lemon zest in the bowl of a food processor fitted with the metal blade. Process, using quick on and off turns, to just barely mince and combine.

Scrape the mixture from the processor bowl into a clean container. Add the oil and vinegar and stir to blend. Season with salt and pepper to taste and serve. Chimichurri can be stored, covered, in the refrigerator for up to 1 day, but the longer you store it, the darker the color will be, and you want it to be a fresh green.

*Nutritional Analysis per Serving (1 tablespoon): calories 168, carbohydrates 2 g, fiber 1 g, protein 1 g, fat 19 g, sodium 103 mg, sugar 0 g*

# Tapenade

MAKES 2 CUPS

This pungent mix is a typical Provençal dish that in France is generally served on small toasts along with an aperitif. I find it works marvels with raw or lightly steamed vegetables. It can also be used to stuff poultry or pork. Tapenade traditionally has anchovies, but I've made them optional here. Either way, it is a tasty dip.

6 tablespoons extra-virgin olive oil

2 tablespoons finely chopped onion

1 tablespoon minced garlic

½ cup chopped red bell pepper

½ cup chopped yellow bell pepper

½ cup chopped green bell pepper

1 cup chopped imported black olives

¾ cup chopped walnuts

3 tablespoons chopped fresh flat-leaf parsley

1 tablespoon minced fresh basil

1 tablespoon chopped capers

¼ cup red wine vinegar

½ cup minced anchovies, optional

Salt and pepper

Heat the oil in a heavy-bottomed saucepan over medium heat. Add the onion and garlic and cook, stirring, just until they begin to color, about 3 minutes. Add the bell peppers and cook, stirring occasionally, just until the peppers have softened, about 6 minutes more.

Stir in the olives, walnuts, parsley, basil, and capers. When blended, add the vinegar and anchovies (if using) and season with salt and pepper to taste.

Lower the heat and cook until the flavors have blended and the mixture is slightly thick, about 5 minutes.

Remove from the heat and set aside to cool. Use immediately, or cover and store in the refrigerator for up to 3 weeks.

*Nutritional Analysis per Serving (2 tablespoons): calories 52, carbohydrates 1 g, fiber 0 g, protein 1 g, fat 5 g, sodium 113 mg, sugar 0 g*

# Creole Crunch

Creole food, which is considered a bit more refined than Cajun, combines zesty French, African, and Spanish flavors. This crunchy rub adds a bit of spice and heat to pork, chicken, steaks, and burgers as well as to shrimp and fish. If you like even more heat, add additional cayenne pepper.

1 cup dried onion flakes

½ cup dried bell pepper flakes

3 tablespoons hot paprika

3 tablespoons dried thyme

3 tablespoons dried oregano

3 tablespoons black pepper

2 tablespoons cayenne pepper

2 tablespoons celery seeds

1 tablespoon dried garlic flakes

Combine all of the ingredients in a small bowl, mixing to blend well. Transfer to an airtight container, cover, and store in a cool, dry spot for up to 6 months.

*Nutritional Analysis per Serving (1 tablespoon): calories 13, carbohydrates 3 g, fiber 1 g, protein 1 g, fat 0 g, sodium 2 mg, sugar 1 g*

# BREAKFAST

I HAVE FOUND THAT making breakfast is one of the most difficult adjustments for people new to the *Grain Brain* diet. This is mostly because so many have, for years, begun their day with a hot drink and some type of bread, without any thought to proper nutrition. The hale and hearty farm breakfast of America's early years simply doesn't exist anymore and, even if it did, it would probably now contain foods high in gluten and carbohydrates. Eggs and bacon have been so maligned that everyone has become afraid to consume them; I insist that eggs, nature's perfect food, be on the table daily. The foods that start your day will set the right tone for the rest of your life.

I am going to give you some extraordinary alternatives to that cuppa and muffin that you have been grabbing and eating on the go. At the *Grain Brain* breakfast table, nuts, eggs, seeds, vegetables, and meat are now going to be part of every morning's start.

# Morning Wake-Up Call

SERVES 1

There's no better way to start the day than with an energy boost. Quick to prepare, smooth to drink, and filled with goodness, this creamy green juice brightens the morning rush. The juice is smoother when processed in a juicer but also works just fine in a blender. It is particularly important that you use organically grown, well-washed ingredients. Feel free to use a regular lemon if a Meyer lemon is not available.

---

8 large kale leaves

4 celery ribs

1 seedless cucumber

1 (1-inch) piece ginger root

1 avocado, peeled, pitted, and chopped

Juice of $\frac{1}{2}$ Meyer lemon

---

Place all of the ingredients in an electric juicer and process to juice. Alternatively, chop the kale, celery, cucumber, and ginger and place them in a blender. Add the avocado and the juice of the half lemon and process on high until smooth. Drink immediately.

*Nutritional Analysis per Serving: calories 361, carbohydrates 37 g, fiber 16 g, protein 11 g, fat 23 g, sodium 196 mg, sugar 8 g*

# Rise and Shine Shake

SERVES 1

This shake is a fabulous wake-up in a glass. You can change the flavor and the health benefits if you like by replacing the blueberries with half of an avocado and the almond milk with unsweetened coconut milk. Either way, it's a delicious, nutritious shake.

---

½ cup frozen blueberries

¼ cup almond meal or freshly pulverized almonds

2 tablespoons ground flaxseed

2 tablespoons almond butter

¾ cup cold unsweetened almond milk

2 or 3 ice cubes

---

Combine the blueberries, almond meal, flaxseed, and almond butter in a blender jar. Add the milk and ice cubes and process until it reaches a shake-like consistency. If it's too thick, add cold water or additional almond milk. Drink immediately.

*Nutritional Analysis per Serving: calories 502, carbohydrates 26 g, fiber 12 g, protein 17 g, fat 41 g, sodium 218 mg, sugar 9 g*

# Quick Crunchy Cereal

This recipe is in my book *Grain Brain*, but I thought it should be included here, too, as it meets all of my dietary guidelines and is so easy to put together for a quick and healthy breakfast. You can use any raw, unsalted nut that you like.

½ cup chopped raw, unsalted walnuts

¼ cup unsweetened coconut flakes

⅓ cup fresh berries

⅔ cup unsweetened almond milk

Combine the walnuts, coconut flakes, and berries in a cereal bowl. Add the milk and stir to combine. Serve.

*Nutritional Analysis per Serving: calories 518, carbohydrates 20 g, fiber 8 g, protein 10 g, fat 47 g, sodium 127 mg, sugar 8 g*

# Ungranola

This quasi-cereal mimics granola, but without any grains, it completely meets our breakfast rules. If you don't have clarified butter on hand, coconut oil or extra-virgin olive oil will work just fine. Watch carefully as you bake, as the nuts can quickly turn from golden and toasty to dark and inedible. If you grow to love this mix as a wholesome start to your day, double or triple the recipe and keep it on hand for snacking as well.

---

1 cup chopped raw almonds

1 cup chopped raw cashews

1 cup raw pumpkin seeds

1 cup unsweetened coconut flakes

2 tablespoons flaxseed

1 tablespoon chia seeds

1 teaspoon ground cinnamon

½ teaspoon ground nutmeg

½ teaspoon ground allspice

1 tablespoon stevia powder

3 tablespoons clarified butter (see page 42), ghee, or unsalted butter, melted

---

Preheat the oven to 350°F. Line a baking sheet with parchment paper or a nonstick silicone pan liner and set aside.

Combine the almonds, cashews, pumpkin seeds, coconut flakes, flaxseed, chia seeds, cinnamon, nutmeg, and allspice in a mixing bowl. Stir in the stevia. When well blended, drizzle with the butter and toss to coat.

Pour the mixture onto the prepared baking sheet and, using a spatula, spread it out to an even layer. Place in the preheated oven and bake, stirring occasionally, until nicely toasted and aromatic, about 25 minutes.

Remove the baking sheet from the oven and place it on a wire rack to allow the mixture to cool. When cool, serve or store in a covered container in a cool spot for up to 3 days or in the refrigerator for up to 1 month.

*Nutritional Analysis per Serving (½ cup): calories 457, carbohydrates 15 g, fiber 6 g, protein 13 g, fat 40 g, sodium 11 mg, sugar 3 g*

# Homemade Turkey Sausage

MAKES 6 PATTIES

We don't usually think about making our own breakfast sausage, but we should. It's a cinch to make and can be stored for future use. The mix also makes a wonderful addition to frittatas and quiches, but for the morning rush, I simply fry up a patty along with a couple of scrambled eggs seasoned with chopped scallions and I'm good to go.

---

2 tablespoons extra-virgin olive oil, plus more for frying

1 cup finely chopped onion

1 tablespoon minced garlic

Salt and black pepper

1½ teaspoons chopped fresh sage

1 teaspoon chopped fresh thyme

1 teaspoon chopped fresh flat-leaf parsley

½ teaspoon ground allspice

Cayenne pepper

1¼ pounds ground turkey

---

Heat the 2 tablespoons olive oil in a medium frying pan over medium heat. Add the onion and garlic, season with salt and pepper to taste, and cook, stirring frequently, until very soft and just beginning to color, about 5 minutes. Stir in the sage, thyme, parsley, allspice, and cayenne pepper to taste and continue to cook for another minute. Remove from the heat and set aside to cool.

When the aromatics are cool, place the turkey in a mixing bowl. Add the cooled onion mixture and stir to blend completely.

To taste for proper seasoning, form a teaspoonful of the mixture into a tiny patty and fry it in a bit of olive oil over medium heat until just cooked through. Taste and, if necessary, season the remaining raw mix with additional salt, pepper, herbs, and/or cayenne.

Using your hands, form the raw mixture into 6 patties of equal size. If you're not ready to cook them, place them in a resealable plastic bag, separated by small sheets of waxed paper, and store in the refrigerator for up to 2 days or in the freezer for up to 3 months. (If frozen, thaw overnight in the refrigerator before cooking.)

When ready to cook, heat a slight slick of olive oil in a nonstick frying pan over medium heat. Add the patties and fry, turning occasionally, until cooked through and brown, about 10 minutes (an instant-read thermometer inserted into the center should read 165°F). Serve.

*Nutritional Analysis per Serving (1 patty): calories 255, carbohydrates 3 g, fiber 1 g, protein 26 g, fat 16 g, sodium 183 mg, sugar 1 g*

# Breakfast Hash

SERVES 6

This is my version of an old-fashioned New England "red flannel" hash. It is usually made with corned beef and potatoes, but I think this version is even better than the classic. Traditionally, the hash should be topped with a poached or fried egg. If you choose to add the egg, bake the hash in individual ramekins and then top each serving with an egg and a sprinkle of chopped parsley. You would then have a sensational brunch dish.

---

2 tablespoons extra-virgin olive oil

1 cup finely chopped onion

1 tablespoon minced garlic

Salt and pepper

1 large beet, roasted, peeled, and finely diced

2 cups finely chopped kale

1 pound finely diced cooked roast beef

1 teaspoon gluten-free Worcestershire sauce, optional

¼ cup grated Parmesan cheese

---

Preheat the oven to 375°F.

Heat the oil in a large, oven-safe frying pan over medium heat. Add the onion and garlic, season with salt and pepper to taste, and cook, stirring frequently, until very soft and just beginning to color, about 5 minutes.

Stir in the beet and kale and continue to cook for another minute or two, just until the kale has wilted. Add the beef and the Worcestershire sauce (if using) and stir to blend completely. Taste and, if necessary, adjust the seasoning.

Pat the mixture down to an even layer and sprinkle the top with the cheese. Transfer to the preheated oven and bake until the top is golden brown and crisp, about 20 minutes. Remove from the oven and serve.

*Nutritional Analysis per Serving: calories 261, carbohydrates 7 g, fiber 1 g, protein 24 g, fat 15 g, sodium 239 mg, sugar 2 g*

# Eggs Benedict with Zucchini Pancakes

SERVES 4

How can you have eggs Benedict without the traditional English muffin? you might ask. Well, you just ditch the muffin and place the ham and eggs on a crispy zucchini pancake. A little more work for the cook, but extra pleasure for the diner. I always make more pancakes than I need because people invariably ask for another. I assure you that you'll never go back to that muffin. Of course, if you are short on time, the eggs and sauce can simply be placed on a bed of leafy greens.

For perfect eggs Benedict, featuring eggs with tender whites and runny yolks, you must gently poach the eggs in just barely simmering water. They should never be cooked at a hard simmer or boil or the whites will become tough and the yolks firm. Since there is now much concern about the safety of lightly cooked eggs, I barely poach the eggs and then hold them in a saucepan of very warm water (130°F) for 15 minutes. This method allows the cook to prepare the remaining ingredients as the eggs warm and cook.

---

1 tablespoon white vinegar

4 extra-large eggs, at room temperature

4 slices Canadian bacon

4 Zucchini Pancakes (recipe follows)

1 recipe Easy Hollandaise Sauce (page 42)

1 tablespoon chopped fresh flat-leaf parsley

---

Preheat the oven to 275°F.

Heat about 3 inches of water in a large, shallow saucepan over medium heat until bubbles form around the edge. Add the vinegar.

In another saucepan of similar size, heat 3 inches of water to 130°F on a candy thermometer. Remove from the heat and cover to keep warm.

Working quickly with one egg at a time, carefully break each egg into a small custard cup and then gently slide the egg from the cup into the barely simmering vinegar-water. When all of the eggs have been added, cook until the whites are just set but the yolks are still very loose, about 2 minutes.

Using a slotted spoon, carefully lift the barely cooked eggs, one at a time, and place them into the 130°F water. Cover and let rest for 15 minutes. You should, from time to time, check the temperature of the water. If it falls below 130°F, slowly add enough boiling water to bring the temperature back up.

Place the Canadian bacon in a large nonstick frying pan over medium-high heat. Fry, turning occasionally, until just lightly browned around the edges, about 4 minutes. Remove from the heat and place on a baking sheet in the preheated oven to keep warm if the eggs or pancakes aren't done yet.

Place a warm pancake in the center of each plate and top with a slice of Canadian bacon. Using a slotted spoon, lift the poached eggs, one at a time, from the water and pat gently with a clean kitchen towel to remove excess water. Place an egg on top of the bacon. (If the edges of the eggs are a bit ragged, carefully trim them with a small knife or kitchen scissors.)

Spoon about 3 tablespoons of the hollandaise sauce on top of each egg, sprinkle with chopped parsley, and serve immediately.

**NOTE:** Those on a restricted sodium diet can eliminate the Canadian bacon from the recipe.

*Nutritional Analysis per Serving: calories 485, carbohydrates 6 g, fiber 1 g, protein 16 g, fat 44 g, sodium 858 mg, sugar 2 g*

## *Zucchini Pancakes*

MAKES ABOUT 8 PANCAKES

---

3 large zucchini

1 extra-large egg white

2 tablespoons almond meal

1 teaspoon paprika

Salt and pepper

3 tablespoons clarified butter (see page 42), ghee, or unsalted butter

---

Using either a hand-held grater or a food processor fitted with the shredding blade, shred the zucchini.

Place the shredded zucchini in the center of a large, clean kitchen towel. Bring the sides up and twist hard to express all of the liquid. You may have to do this a few times to get all the liquid out; the drier the zucchini, the crisper the pancakes will be.

Place the shredded, drained zucchini in a large mixing bowl. Add the egg white, almond meal, paprika, and salt and pepper to taste, tossing to blend in the seasonings.

Heat the clarified butter in a large frying pan over medium heat. When very hot but not smoking, spoon in the zucchini mixture to make individual circles about 3½ inches in diameter (you will need to do this in batches). Fry, turning once, until cooked through, golden brown, and crisp, about 5 minutes.

Using a spatula, transfer to a double layer of paper towels to drain. If necessary, place on a baking sheet in a low oven to keep warm until ready to serve.

*Nutritional Analysis per Serving (1 pancake): calories 76, carbohydrates 3 g, fiber 1 g, protein 2 g, fat 6 g, sodium 90 mg, sugar 2 g*

# Roasted Onion Omelet with Sun-Dried Tomato and Onion Chutney

SERVES 6

This sensational omelet can be served either hot or at room temperature for breakfast, brunch, lunch, or a light supper. I always try to have some left over because it makes such a tasty addition to green salads for supper. The Indian spices are so aromatic that you need almost nothing else to create a memorable meal. The chutney can also be used as a condiment for grilled meats, poultry, or fish.

---

10 large eggs

¼ cup chopped fresh cilantro

1 teaspoon hot curry powder

½ teaspoon ground toasted cumin

Pinch ground turmeric

Pinch cayenne pepper, or to taste

Salt and pepper

2 tablespoons extra-virgin olive oil

1½ cups roasted onions (see Note)

1 teaspoon roasted garlic puree (see Note)

½ teaspoon minced ginger root

2 cups finely chopped leafy greens, such as kale, mustard greens, or collards

1 cup finely diced peeled and seeded plum tomatoes, well drained

1 cup chopped mushrooms

1 teaspoon minced seeded hot green chile, or to taste

6 tablespoons Sun-Dried Tomato and Onion Chutney (page 66)

---

Break the eggs into a mixing bowl and whisk to blend. Add the cilantro, curry, cumin, turmeric, and cayenne and combine. Season with salt and pepper to taste. Set aside.

Heat the oil in a large, nonstick sauté pan over medium heat. Add the roasted onions, garlic, and ginger and sauté for 2 minutes. Stir in the greens, tomatoes, mushrooms, and chile and sauté until the flavors have combined and the vegetables are very hot, about 5 minutes.

Pour the seasoned eggs into the pan, lifting and tilting the pan so that the eggs cover the vegetables. Reduce the heat to medium-low and cover. Cook until the eggs are set and the bottom is brown, about 12 minutes. (You can turn the omelet if you wish to brown both sides, but it is not necessary.) Alternatively, you can bake the omelet in an oven-safe skillet at 350°F for about 45 minutes.

Flip the cooked omelet onto a warm serving platter. Cut into six wedges, dollop 1 tablespoon chutney on each, and serve immediately.

**NOTE:** To make 1½ cups roasted onions, combine 4 cups diced onions with ¼ cup olive oil and season with salt and pepper to taste. Spread out in a nonstick baking pan and place in a preheated 350°F oven. Roast, tossing occasionally, until the onions are golden brown and most of the moisture has cooked out, about 30 minutes. Use immediately, or cover and store in the refrigerator for up to 1 week. Roasted onions may be added to other egg dishes or used as a flavoring accent for other vegetables or sauces.

To make roasted garlic: If roasting a whole head, lay the head on its side and cut about ⅛ inch off the stem end. Lightly coat the entire head (or individual unpeeled cloves) with olive oil. Wrap tightly in aluminum foil and place in a baking pan in a preheated 350°F oven. Roast until soft and aromatic; whole heads should take about 25 minutes and individual cloves about 12 minutes. Remove from the oven, unwrap, and let cool slightly. Using your fingertips, push the flesh from the skin. The clove may or may not pop out whole, but either way it doesn't matter, as roasted garlic usually gets mashed or pureed before use. Use immediately, or cover and store in the refrigerator for up to 1 week or in the freezer for up to 3 months.

*Nutritional Analysis per Serving: calories 325, carbohydrates 20 g, fiber 4 g, protein 14 g, fat 22 g, sodium 323 mg, sugar 8 g*

## Sun-Dried Tomato and Onion Chutney

MAKES ABOUT 3 CUPS

3 cups chopped sweet onions

2 cups chopped sun-dried tomatoes (not oil-packed)

2 tablespoons minced ginger root

1 tablespoon minced seeded hot red or green chile

1 tablespoon stevia powder

1 tablespoon chili powder

2 teaspoons mustard seeds

1 teaspoon cumin seeds

½ cup cider vinegar

1 tablespoon freshly squeezed lemon juice

Combine the onions, tomatoes, ginger, and chile in a heavy-bottomed saucepan (preferably nonstick). Stir in the stevia, chili powder, mustard seeds, and cumin seeds. Add the vinegar and lemon juice and stir to combine. Place over medium heat and cook, stirring frequently, until the onions are very soft and the mixture is quite thick and has a well-balanced flavor, about 30 minutes. If the mixture gets too thick before the onions have softened, add water or tomato juice, ¼ cup at a time, to thin.

Remove from the heat and allow to come to room temperature. Serve, or cover and store in the refrigerator for up to 1 month.

*Nutritional Analysis per Serving (1 tablespoon): calories 15, carbohydrates 3 g, fiber 1 g, protein 1 g, fat 0 g, sodium 4 mg, sugar 1 g*

# Manchego Tortilla

No, no, no—this is not the tortilla you are thinking of. In Spain, an omelet is known as a tortilla and the traditional *tortilla de patatas* contains potatoes, which I have eliminated to make this a *Grain Brain* favorite. Prepared in a pan specially made to create a soft, juicy finished cake about 12 inches around and 1½ inches high, this classic Spanish dish can be found in tapas bars throughout Spain.

When making this tortilla, it is most important to prepare it in a nonstick, oven-safe pan with a good amount of spicy extra-virgin olive oil (see Note). For extra Spanish flavor, add about 1½ cups chopped free-range, organic chorizo when you are sautéing the leeks and garlic.

If you can't find Manchego cheese, you can substitute Asiago or a very sharp white cheddar.

⅓ cup spicy extra-virgin olive oil

1½ cups chopped leeks, white part only

1 teaspoon minced garlic

Salt and pepper

3 cups roughly chopped well-drained artichoke hearts (jarred, canned, or thawed frozen)

8 large eggs

¾ cup chopped Manzanilla olives

6 ounces thinly sliced Manchego cheese

Preheat the oven to 350°F.

Heat the olive oil in a 12-inch nonstick oven-safe frying pan over medium heat. Add the leeks and garlic. Season with salt and pepper to taste and sauté just until the leeks are softened, about 4 minutes. Add the artichoke hearts and cook for an additional 2 minutes. Remove from the heat and, using the back of a spatula, pat the artichoke mixture evenly into the pan.

Combine the eggs and olives, whisking to blend very well. Pour half of the egg mixture over the artichoke mixture; it should just barely cover it. Lay about two-thirds of the cheese over the top and then pour the remaining egg mixture into the pan. Transfer to the preheated oven and bake until well set and beginning to brown, about 15 minutes.

Remove from the oven and cover the top with the remaining cheese. Return to the oven and continue to bake until the cheese has melted and browned, about 15 minutes more.

Again, remove the pan from the oven and place it on a wire rack to rest for 5 minutes. Then, invert the tortilla onto a serving plate, cut into six wedges, and serve hot or at room temperature.

**NOTE:** A green, acidic, spicy extra-virgin olive oil can be found only by asking your shopkeeper which of the fine olive oils can be classified as such. Often, specialty markets or Italian food stores will have samples available for tasting, which is, by far, the best way to find an olive oil that appeals to your palate.

*Nutritional Analysis per Serving: calories 399, carbohydrates 15 g, fiber 8 g, protein 18 g, fat 31 g, sodium 658 mg, sugar 2 g*

# Torta Rustica

SERVES 6

This torta is a hearty breakfast and also makes a terrific brunch or lunch dish when served with a fresh spinach salad on the side. A traditional Italian holiday torta is usually encased in pastry dough. My version is lighter and easier to make—and perhaps even tastier than its Italian cousin.

3 tablespoons extra-virgin olive oil

½ cup grated onion

1 teaspoon minced garlic

2 cups cooked, chopped, well-drained spinach (see Note)

1 cup sheep's milk ricotta cheese

½ cup grated Pecorino Romano cheese

Salt and pepper

Preheat the oven to 500°F. Generously butter a 2-quart casserole and set aside.

Heat the olive oil in a small frying pan over medium heat. Add the onion and garlic and sauté just until softened, about 3 minutes. Remove from the heat and set aside.

Combine the spinach with the ricotta and Pecorino in a mixing bowl. Add the reserved onion mixture, season with salt and pepper to taste, and stir to blend completely. Scrape the mixture into the prepared casserole, smoothing the top with a spatula.

Transfer to the preheated oven and bake for 5 minutes; then, lower the heat to 350°F and bake until completely set and golden brown around the edges, about 20 minutes more.

Remove from the oven and set aside for 5 minutes. Cut into six wedges and serve.

**NOTE:** You can use frozen chopped organic spinach if you thaw it completely and carefully squeeze out all of the liquid. If the spinach is too wet, the torta won't set properly.

*Nutritional Analysis per Serving: calories 222, carbohydrates 11 g, fiber 2 g, protein 14 g, fat 20 g, sodium 338 mg, sugar 2 g*

# LUNCH

---

IF YOU NORMALLY EAT lunch in a restaurant or company cafeteria, now is the time to start brown-bagging it. Although you can often find unadulterated dishes to order when you eat out, it's far better to lunch on something you've made at home using the best possible ingredients. Soups and stews can often be eaten at room temperature or packed in a thermos; salads can be put together and dressed when you are ready to eat; and many of the more complicated dishes can be made for a lunch or brunch or even dinner at home and then the leftovers used to create a healthy lunch for the next day. I can almost guarantee that if you share your brown bag with your co-workers you will soon have everyone following your diet.

# Really Great Tomato Soup

SERVES 6

Perfectly ripe, juicy tomatoes give this soup the intense flavor you need; big, fat, deep-red beefsteaks are the best. If there are fresh herbs that you particularly like, add them to the onions or use them as a garnish. Basil, of course, is the perfect mate for ripe tomatoes. A slice or two of fresh green chile will add a bit of heat if that's to your liking.

½ cup unsalted butter

8 ounces onions, chopped

1 teaspoon minced garlic

6 pounds very ripe tomatoes, cored and chopped

Salt and pepper

Crumbled feta cheese, for optional garnish

Heat the butter in a large nonreactive soup pot over medium heat. Add the onions and garlic, lower the heat, and cook, stirring frequently, until soft and fragrant but not colored, about 20 minutes.

Add the tomatoes and season with salt and pepper to taste. Raise the heat to medium-low and continue to cook, stirring frequently, until the tomatoes are mushy and the mixture soupy, about 25 minutes.

Remove from the heat. Transfer to a blender, in batches if necessary, and process until smooth. Be sure to hold down the lid of the blender with a kitchen towel, as the pressure from the hot liquid can force it right off.

When all of the soup has been pureed, pour it through a fine-mesh sieve into a clean nonreactive saucepan. Taste and, if necessary, season with additional salt and pepper. Return to medium heat and cook until hot.

Remove from the heat and ladle into shallow soup bowls. Sprinkle with feta cheese, if desired, and serve.

*Nutritional Analysis per Serving (about 1½ cups): calories 224, carbohydrates 20 g, fiber 6 g, protein 4 g, fat 16 g, sodium 409 mg, sugar 13 g*

# Mushroom-Hazelnut Soup

SERVES 6

When I first tasted this soup I experienced an intriguing mix of flavors on my palate. It is a trickster—you get a hint of hazelnut, but when the nuts blend into the mushrooms a unique umami flavor is revealed. You can make it with either chicken stock for a rich soup or vegetable stock for a lighter lunch. If you need only one serving, it keeps well, covered and refrigerated, and will taste even better when warmed up a day or two later. If you want to move it to the dinner table, top it with slices of grilled pork sausage and a mound of fried thinly sliced shiitake mushrooms, along with a garnish of chopped flat-leaf parsley or tarragon.

¼ cup unsalted butter

1 pound onions, sliced

1¼ pounds cremini mushrooms, chopped

Salt and pepper

3 to 4 cups chicken stock (page 33) or low-sodium chicken broth

½ cup finely ground toasted hazelnuts (from about 3 ounces whole nuts)

Heat the butter in a large saucepan over medium-low heat. Add the onions and cook, stirring frequently, until soft and translucent, about 12 minutes. Add the mushrooms and continue to cook, stirring frequently, for 10 minutes. Season with salt and pepper to taste. Add enough chicken stock to barely cover, raise the heat, and bring to a simmer. Immediately reduce the heat and simmer for an additional 10 minutes.

Remove from the heat and stir in the nuts. Pour into a blender, in batches if necessary, and process until smooth. You may have to add more chicken stock to reach a smooth soup consistency. Be sure to hold down the lid of the blender with a kitchen towel, as the pressure from the hot liquid can force the lid right off.

Pour the soup into a clean saucepan and place over medium heat until very hot. Remove from the heat and serve.

*Nutritional Analysis per Serving (about 1 cup): calories 198, carbohydrates 14 g, fiber 3 g, protein 6 g, fat 15 g, sodium 41 mg, sugar 5 g*

# Winter Squash Soup

SERVES 6

This soup is perfect for a fall or winter day when there is a chill in the air, with the heat from the ginger and chile balancing the sweetness of the squash. It also makes a beautiful first course for a dinner party, pale orange highlighted with a few dots of heavy cream and chives as garnish. The soup may be made ahead of time and stored, covered, in the refrigerator for up to 3 days or in the freezer for up to 2 months.

Since this soup is relatively high in carbohydrates, take care about the remainder of your total carbohydrate intake for the day.

---

2 medium winter squash, such as butternut, kabocha, or Hubbard, peeled, halved, seeded, and cubed

1 cup chopped shallots

1 teaspoon grated ginger root

1 teaspoon minced seeded green chile

½ teaspoon curry powder

¼ teaspoon ground nutmeg

¼ teaspoon ground cinnamon

¼ teaspoon ground cardamom

Salt and white pepper

5 cups chicken stock (page 33) or low-sodium chicken broth

2 tablespoons heavy cream, for optional garnish

1 tablespoon minced fresh chives or flat-leaf parsley, for optional garnish

---

Set a steamer basket in a large stockpot with just enough water to come up to the bottom of the steamer basket. Bring the water to a boil over high heat. Combine the squash cubes, shallots, and ginger in the steamer basket, cover, and steam until the squash is very tender, about 15 minutes.

Transfer the squash mixture, in batches, to a food processor fitted with the metal blade. Process to a smooth puree. As the squash is pureed, transfer it to a large saucepan.

When all of the squash is pureed, add the chile, curry powder, nutmeg, cinnamon, and cardamom to the pan, along with salt and white pepper to taste. Add the chicken stock and place over medium-high heat. Bring to a simmer; then, lower the heat and simmer until the flavors have blended, about 20 minutes.

Serve hot, garnished with just a few dots of heavy cream and a sprinkle of chopped chives or flat-leaf parsley, if desired.

*Nutritional Analysis per Serving (2 cups): calories 162, carbohydrates 39 g, fiber 7 g, protein 5 g, fat 0 g, sodium 170 mg, sugar 9 g*

# Chilled Avocado Soup

SERVES 2

This soup is delicious unadorned, but if you feel like getting fancy, a little mound of crab or lobster meat, a beautiful large shrimp, or even a few pieces of avocado in the center make it dinner-party ready. It is light and refreshing, and the beneficial avocado makes it a star in the *Grain Brain* diet.

I've made the recipe for only two servings so that it remains a glorious pale green. If you are serving more than two people it can easily be doubled or tripled, but it can't sit around for very long as the color darkens and isn't nearly as pleasing.

---

1 large ripe avocado, peeled, pitted, and diced

½ cup diced peeled seedless cucumber

1½ cups cold chicken stock (page 33) or low-sodium chicken broth

¼ cup cold unsweetened almond milk

2 tablespoons freshly squeezed lime juice

Salt

Tabasco sauce

Chopped mint leaves, for optional garnish

---

Place the avocado and cucumber in a blender jar. Add the chicken stock, almond milk, and lime juice and process until smooth. Pour into a bowl and season with salt and Tabasco to taste.

Serve immediately, garnished with chopped mint, if desired, or cover and refrigerate for no more than 3 hours or the soup will begin to discolor.

*Nutritional Analysis per Serving: calories 166, carbohydrates 10 g, fiber 6 g, protein 4 g, fat 14 g, sodium 380 mg, sugar 1 g*

# Coconut-Chicken Soup

SERVES 6

Here's another elementary soup that makes a delicious and quick lunch. Most Asian markets carry kaffir lime leaves and lemongrass, but don't panic if you can't find them—I've given substitutions that still make it doable. And you can substitute shrimp or salmon for the chicken if you like.

---

3½ cups chicken stock (page 33) or low-sodium chicken broth

2 tablespoons Red Boat fish sauce *(nam pla)* (see Note)

2 tablespoons freshly squeezed lemon juice

1 tablespoon freshly squeezed lime juice

6 kaffir lime leaves (fresh or thawed frozen) *or* the zest of
   1 lime plus 2 bay leaves

1 cup peeled, seeded, diced tomato

1 tablespoon minced lemongrass (fresh or thawed frozen) *or*
   1 strip lemon peel plus a few flat-leaf parsley stems

3 (⅛-inch-thick) slices ginger root

1 tablespoon minced seeded red or green chile, or to taste

1½ cups unsweetened coconut milk

1 large boneless, skinless chicken breast, cut into thin strips

1 bunch enoki mushrooms, tough stems removed

3 tablespoons chopped fresh cilantro

1 tablespoon chopped fresh mint

---

Combine the chicken stock, fish sauce, and lemon and lime juices in a large saucepan. Add the kaffir lime leaves, tomato, lemongrass, ginger, and chile and bring to a simmer over medium heat. Add the coconut milk, chicken strips, and mushrooms. Return to the simmer and cook until the chicken is just cooked through, about 7 minutes—be careful not to overcook. Do not allow the soup to come to a boil or the broth will separate slightly.

Remove from the heat and stir in the cilantro and mint. Serve immediately.

**NOTE:** Red Boat brand fish sauce is 100 percent gluten-free (which is not the case with many other fish sauces), but note that it is high in sodium.

*Nutritional Analysis per Serving (1¼ cups): calories 210, carbohydrates 5 g, fiber 1 g, protein 20 g, fat 12 g, sodium 563 mg, sugar 1 g*

# Texas-Style Chili

SERVES 6

In Texas, unlike other parts of America, real chili does not contain beans. This is about as pure a Texas chili as you can get—one that could have been found out on the range during a cattle run. You can serve it with some freshly chopped red onions, cilantro, and hot chiles as toppings to take the flavor up a notch or two if you wish. For an even richer flavor, an ounce of dark (over 70 percent cacao) chocolate added with the meat will add intensity and depth.

---

2 cups water

7 dried chiles, such as a mix of ancho, pasilla, and guajillo, seeded

6 tablespoons clarified butter (see page 42), ghee, or unsalted butter

2 pounds coarsely chopped beef stew meat

Salt and pepper

2 cups diced onion

2 tablespoons minced garlic

1 tablespoon minced seeded jalapeño chile, or to taste

1 tablespoon ground cumin

1 teaspoon dried oregano

5 cups beef stock (page 33) or low-sodium beef broth

2 tablespoons chopped fresh cilantro

1 tablespoon freshly squeezed lime juice

½ cup grated queso fresco or other dry, crumbly white cheese

---

Combine the water and dried chiles in a medium saucepan over high heat. Bring to a boil; then, lower the heat and simmer, stirring occasionally, until the chiles are very soft, about 10 minutes. Remove from the heat and set aside to cool slightly.

Pour the chiles and about half of the cooking liquid into a blender and process to make a thick puree, adding more liquid as necessary to achieve the right consistency.

Heat the butter in a large saucepan over medium-high heat. Add the beef, season with salt and pepper to taste, and fry, stirring frequently, just until brown, about 5 minutes. Using a slotted spoon, transfer the meat to a bowl.

To the hot pan, add the onion, garlic, jalapeño, cumin, and oregano and cook, stirring frequently, until just beginning to brown, about 6 minutes. Add the reserved dried chile puree and cook, stirring frequently, until very dark and quite thick, about 4 minutes. Take care that the mixture does not scorch on the bottom of the pan.

Stir in the reserved beef, along with the stock. Bring to a boil and then lower the heat and simmer until reduced by half and very thick, about 1 hour.

Remove from the heat and stir in the cilantro and lime juice. Taste and, if necessary, season with additional salt and pepper. Serve, sprinkled with the cheese.

*Nutritional Analysis per Serving: calories 606, carbohydrates 18 g, fiber 6 g, protein 45 g, fat 40 g, sodium 598 mg, sugar 4 g*

# Curried Pork Stew

SERVES 4

This quick and uncomplicated lunch stew keeps, covered and refrigerated, for a few days, so if you only need lunch for one, make it anyway—it will be a fast reheat for lunch later in the week or a tasty side dish for grilled fish or poultry at dinnertime.

---

2 tablespoons coconut oil

12 ounces lean pork, cut into small cubes

2 cups chopped onion

1 tablespoon minced garlic

1 teaspoon minced seeded jalapeño or other hot green chile, or to taste

1 tablespoon hot curry powder

1/4 teaspoon cayenne pepper

Pinch ground turmeric

1 (6-ounce) bag or 1 (11-ounce) bunch spinach, tough stems removed

3½ cups unsweetened coconut milk

Salt

---

Heat the oil in a large saucepan over medium heat. When hot but not smoking, add the pork, onion, garlic, and chile, stirring to combine. Fry, stirring frequently, until the pork has cooked through and the aromatics have softened, about 6 minutes; then, sprinkle in the curry, cayenne, and turmeric and stir to incorporate.

Add the spinach and, using tongs, toss to coat the spinach with the onion mixture. Stir in the coconut milk, season with salt to taste, and bring to a simmer. Remove from the heat and serve.

*Nutritional Analysis per Serving: calories 612, carbohydrates 22 g, fiber 4 g, protein 23 g, fat 49 g, sodium 454 mg, sugar 4 g*

# Green Mango, Watercress, and Arugula Salad

SERVES 6

The tongue-tingling chiles and peppery greens contrast beautifully with the sweet-tartness of mango, making for a refreshing salad. The popularity of Thai cooking has brought green mangos to many supermarkets, but if you can't find them, substitute jicama or underripe pears.

---

2 teaspoons stevia powder

Juice of 3 limes

1 teaspoon toasted sesame oil

4 red birds' eye chiles or other small, hot red chiles, seeded and minced

Salt

10 ounces watercress sprigs, tough ends removed

3 ounces baby arugula

2 large green mangos, peeled and cut into julienne strips

1 tablespoon black sesame seeds, optional

---

Place the stevia in a small nonstick saucepan over low heat. Cook, stirring frequently, just until it has melted completely, about a minute. Remove from the heat and whisk in the lime juice and sesame oil. Add the chiles and stir to combine. Season with salt to taste. Set aside to cool.

Combine the watercress and arugula in a large mixing bowl. Toss the mango strips with the greens. Pour the cooled sauce over the top and toss to combine.

Mound equal portions of the salad in the center of each of six salad plates. Sprinkle with sesame seeds, if desired, and serve.

*Nutritional Analysis per Serving: calories 55, carbohydrates 11 g, fiber 1 g, protein 2 g, fat 1 g, sodium 614 mg, sugar 8 g*

# Avocado-Walnut Salad

SERVES 2

Throughout the Middle East you will find salads made with a combination of nuts and fruits or vegetables. This is one of my favorites. Just be sure to toast the walnuts, as that will give them the extra crunch they need to offset the creamy avocado.

Since this salad is relatively high in carbohydrates, take care about the remainder of your total carbohydrate intake for the day.

⅔ cup diced celery root or celery

⅔ cup diced seedless cucumber

½ cup chopped toasted walnuts, plus more for optional garnish

¼ cup finely diced Vidalia onion

1 avocado, peeled, pitted, and cut into chunks

½ cup Spiced Vinaigrette (page 38) or vinaigrette of your choice

1 head romaine lettuce, cut lengthwise into long, thin strips

Toss together the celery root, cucumber, walnuts, and onion in a medium mixing bowl. Add the avocado and, using about half of the vinaigrette, lightly dress the mix.

Place the romaine on a serving plate and dress with the remaining vinaigrette. Mound the avocado salad on top and serve, garnished with additional toasted walnuts, if desired.

*Nutritional Analysis per Serving: calories 832, carbohydrates 36 g, fiber 77 g, protein 16 g, fat 77 g, sodium 313 mg, sugar 11 g*

# Caesar Salad with Asiago Tuiles

SERVES 2

If you go the extra distance and make the Asiago *tuiles* (just a fancy French name for a thin wafer), you will never miss the croutons that usually garnish a Caesar salad. For a more substantial lunch, top each serving with a poached egg garnished with two additional anchovy fillets.

Salt

1 garlic clove, peeled

1 head romaine lettuce, chopped

1 large egg yolk, beaten

¼ cup freshly squeezed lemon juice

1 tablespoon white wine vinegar

1 teaspoon dry mustard

1 cup extra-virgin olive oil

3 anchovy fillets, well drained and chopped

¼ cup grated Parmesan cheese

1 tablespoon minced capers

White pepper

4 Asiago *Tuiles* (recipe follows)

Sprinkle about a tablespoon of salt into a wooden salad bowl. Using the garlic clove, rub the salt into the bowl so that it is seasoned with garlic. Discard the garlic, wipe the salt out of the bowl, and add the lettuce.

Combine the egg yolk, lemon juice, vinegar, and dry mustard in a blender and process to blend. With the motor running, slowly add the oil through the hole in the lid, processing until well emulsified.

Pour the dressing into a small bowl and whisk in the anchovies, cheese, and capers. Taste and adjust the seasoning with salt and white pepper.

Pour just enough of the dressing over the lettuce to lightly coat and toss to combine. Serve with the Asiago *tuiles* (2 per person) on the side.

*Nutritional Analysis per Serving: calories 346, carbohydrates 12 g, fiber 7 g, protein 12 g, fat 30 g, sodium 489 mg, sugar 4 g*

## *Asiago Tuiles*

MAKES 8 *TUILES*

---

½ cup grated Asiago (or Parmesan) cheese

---

Preheat the oven to 325°F. Line a baking sheet with parchment paper.

Place a 2-inch round cookie cutter on the parchment paper and sprinkle an even layer of cheese (about 1 tablespoon) inside the circle. Continue making cheese circles, leaving about 2 inches between each one, until you have made eight. You will need only four, but you may have some breakage, plus they are a delicious snack.

Place the baking sheet in the preheated oven. Bake until the cheese circles have melted into 2-inch solid disks, about 4 minutes. Remove from the oven and set aside to cool.

Using a spatula, carefully remove the disks from the baking sheet, keeping them whole. Do take care because the disks are quite fragile. If not using immediately, store in an airtight container, separated by waxed paper, at room temperature for up to 1 day.

# Tomatoes with Mozzarella, Avocado, and Basil

SERVES 2

This is a bit more substantial than the usual caprese salad as it has avocado in the mix. The buffalo mozzarella adds a milky richness that melds right into the creamy avocado.

---

2 ripe tomatoes, cored and thinly sliced crosswise

8 ounces fresh buffalo mozzarella

1 large avocado, peeled, pitted, and thinly sliced

¼ cup extra-virgin olive oil

2 tablespoons red wine vinegar

Salt and pepper

2 tablespoons chopped fresh basil

---

Lay alternating slices of tomato, mozzarella, and avocado around the outside edge of each of two luncheon plates. You should have enough remaining to make a second circle in the center of the plate. Drizzle with olive oil and a few splashes of vinegar. Season with salt and pepper to taste and sprinkle the basil over all. Serve immediately.

*Nutritional Analysis per Serving: calories 775, carbohydrates 20 g, fiber 9 g, protein 28 g, fat 77 g, sodium 121 mg, sugar 6 g*

# Greek Salad

SERVES 4

The better the tomatoes, the better this salad. You want them ripe, juicy, and straight off the vine for maximum flavor. Of course, it would be best if you could walk out the door and pick them from your garden—don't we all wish this were so? I like meaty Greek olives in the salad, although in Greece this would be a no-no, as olives are usually eaten as a side dish there.

---

2 ripe tomatoes, cored and cut into chunks

1 medium seedless cucumber, peeled and cut into chunks

1 small red onion, cut lengthwise into slivers

1 cup diced sheep's milk feta cheese

½ cup pitted Greek olives

2 teaspoons capers

¼ cup Italian Vinaigrette (page 37)

6 cups chopped romaine lettuce

1 teaspoon dried oregano

---

Combine the tomatoes, cucumber, and onion in a mixing bowl. Add the cheese, olives, and capers, tossing gently to blend. Drizzle with the vinaigrette and again toss to coat.

Place an equal portion of the lettuce on each of four luncheon plates. Mound the tomato salad on top. Sprinkle with oregano and serve.

*Nutritional Analysis per Serving: calories 319, carbohydrates 21 g, fiber 10 g, protein 13 g, fat 24 g, sodium 794 mg, sugar 8 g*

# Chef's Salad Bowl

SERVES 4

This is a complete meal in a bowl and comes together quickly, once you learn to start keeping hard-boiled eggs on hand for a little snack or pick-me-up. You should always serve a chef's salad with the ingredients beautifully arranged on top and toss it at the last minute.

---

6 cups roughly chopped crisp lettuce, such as romaine or iceberg

⅓ cup Basic Vinaigrette (page 35)

4 ounces rare roast beef, cut into strips

8 ounces turkey breast, cut into strips

4 ounces Swiss cheese, cut into strips

4 ounces cheddar cheese, cut into strips

2 large hard-boiled eggs, peeled and quartered (see Note)

4 ripe plum tomatoes, peeled, cored, and thinly sliced crosswise

1 avocado, peeled, pitted, and thinly sliced

2 radishes, thinly sliced

---

Place the lettuce in a large wooden salad bowl. Drizzle about half of the vinaigrette over the top and toss to lightly coat.

Arrange the roast beef in a circle around the edge of the salad bowl. Then, moving inward, make a circle of turkey. Place the Swiss and cheddar cheeses in equal mounds in the center of the ring of meats.

Place the egg quarters equidistant around the edge of the roast beef. Then, place a circle of tomato and avocado between the roast beef and turkey, followed by a circle of radish between the turkey and the cheeses.

After presenting at the table, toss and serve immediately, with the extra dressing on the side.

**NOTE:** To make perfect hard-boiled eggs, place the eggs in a saucepan with cold water to cover by at least an inch. Place over high heat and bring to a boil. Immediately remove the pan from the heat and cover. Let stand for 15 minutes; then, drain off the hot water and place the pan under cold running water. Continue running cold water until the eggs are cold. Crack the shells in random spots and peel, from the larger end down, under cold running water.

*Nutritional Analysis per Serving: calories 667, carbohydrates 19 g, fiber 11 g, protein 49 g, fat 46 g, sodium 396 mg, sugar 6 g*

# Tuscan Salad

SERVES 4

The Tuscan hills are the backdrop for this very tasty salad, mainly because that is where you will find one of the oldest and largest breeds of cattle still being bred—the Chianina. Their meat is highly prized for its richness and nutritional value; of course, the most highly prized animals are grass-fed, just as they were centuries ago. When you are not in Tuscany, any of our American grass-fed beef will be an excellent substitute.

---

1 pound cubed cooked roast beef

1 red onion, peeled and cut into thin strips

1 large ripe tomato, cored, seeded, and chopped

¼ cup chopped anchovies

¼ cup Balsamic Vinaigrette (page 36)

8 cups mixed bitter greens, such as chicory, arugula, escarole, and radicchio

¼ cup torn basil leaves

2 tablespoons capers, optional

---

Place the beef in a mixing bowl. Add the onion, tomato, and anchovies, stirring to combine. Add the vinaigrette, tossing to lightly coat.

Combine the bitter greens with the basil on a serving platter, tossing to blend. Scoop the beef mixture over the greens. Sprinkle with capers, if desired, and serve.

**VARIATIONS:** The salad can be made with roast pork, chicken, or turkey instead of beef.

*Nutritional Analysis per Serving: calories 386, carbohydrates 8 g, fiber 3 g, protein 35 g, fat 25 g, sodium 447 mg, sugar 2 g*

# Beef and Watercress Salad

Just a tad spicy, but a first-rate combo—fatty beef, herbaceous watercress, zesty citrus, topped off with fragrant fresh herbs and crunchy bits of coconut. Who could ask for more?

---

1 pound rare roast beef, cut into $\frac{1}{2}$-inch-thick strips

2 bunches watercress, tough stems removed

1 medium red onion, thinly sliced

1 cup sliced radishes

$\frac{1}{3}$ cup melted coconut oil

2 tablespoons freshly squeezed lime juice

1 teaspoon chili powder

1 teaspoon minced garlic

$\frac{1}{4}$ teaspoon cayenne pepper

$\frac{1}{4}$ cup toasted coconut flakes

$\frac{1}{4}$ cup fresh cilantro leaves

$\frac{1}{4}$ cup fresh mint leaves

---

Combine the beef, watercress, onion, and radishes in a large mixing bowl.

Whisk together the oil and juice in a small bowl. When blended, whisk in the chili powder, garlic, and cayenne. Pour the dressing over the beef mixture, tossing to evenly coat.

Scoop the salad onto a serving plate and sprinkle the coconut, cilantro, and mint over the top. Serve immediately.

*Nutritional Analysis per Serving: calories 468, carbohydrates 5 g, fiber 1 g, protein 31 g, fat 34 g, sodium 54 mg, sugar 2 g*

# Thai Pork Lettuce Cups

SERVES 4

This zesty mix makes a light and refreshing lunch that is painless to put together. It can be served on a bed of lettuce leaves, as I suggest here, but it can also be wrapped in lettuce leaves for gluten-free spring rolls. Ground chicken, turkey, or lamb may be substituted for the pork.

---

1 tablespoon coconut oil

1 pound lean ground pork

2 tablespoons minced shallot

1 tablespoon minced garlic

2 tablespoons minced red onion

2 tablespoons minced fresh mint

1 tablespoon minced scallion

1 tablespoon minced fresh cilantro

1 tablespoon minced seeded hot red chile, or to taste

1 tablespoon freshly squeezed lime juice

1 tablespoon Red Boat fish sauce (*nam pla;* see page 81)

Salt

12 large Boston lettuce leaves

4 mint sprigs, for garnish

---

Heat the oil in a large frying pan over medium heat. Add the pork, shallot, and garlic and fry, stirring frequently, until the pork is crumbly and cooked through, about 8 minutes.

Remove from the heat and scrape into a mixing bowl. Add the onion, mint, scallion, cilantro, and chile, stirring to blend. Add the lime juice and fish sauce and blend well. Taste and, if necessary, season with salt.

Place 3 lettuce leaves in the center of each of four luncheon plates. Mound an equal portion of the pork mixture into the center of each. Garnish with a mint sprig and serve.

*Nutritional Analysis per Serving: calories 267, carbohydrates 5 g, fiber 1 g, protein 37 g, fat 11 g, sodium 529 mg, sugar 2 g*

# Warm Rainbow Chard, Pancetta, and Almond Salad

SERVES 4

The warm pancetta and dressing will slightly wilt the chard, keeping it tasting fresh but not quite raw. If you use rainbow chard, the salad is visually appealing, and the combination of soft chard, toasty almonds, and crisp pancetta makes it taste as good as it looks.

---

1 bunch rainbow chard or Swiss chard, tough stems removed and leaves torn into pieces

8 ounces pancetta, diced

2 tablespoons extra-virgin olive oil

3 tablespoons red wine vinegar

1 tablespoon Dijon mustard

Cracked black pepper

1 cup raw almonds, toasted and chopped

---

Place the chard in a large heatproof salad bowl. Set aside.

Place the pancetta and oil in a large frying pan over medium-low heat. Fry, stirring frequently, until all of the fat has rendered out and the pancetta is brown and crisp, about 12 minutes. Remove from the heat. Using a slotted spoon, transfer the pancetta to a double layer of paper towels to drain.

Whisk the vinegar and mustard into the fat in the pan. Season with cracked black pepper to taste. Pour the dressing over the chard and add the almonds and warm pancetta, tossing to combine. Serve while still warm.

**NOTE:** Those on a restricted sodium diet can eliminate the pancetta from the recipe. In this case, heat the olive oil in a small frying pan and proceed with the recipe.

*Nutritional Analysis per Serving: calories 513, carbohydrates 15 g, fiber 6 g, protein 18 g, fat 43 g, sodium 1250 mg, sugar 3 g*

# Tomatoes Stuffed with Shrimp Salad

SERVES 4

When friends gather, this is an exceptional lunch, as it takes no time to prepare but looks as though the cook has spent hours making it. In place of the shrimp, cooked lobster, line-caught tuna, or free-range, organic chicken or turkey will make an equally tasty filling. If you want to fancy it up a bit, make a little avocado salsa to top it off. All that is required is a cup or so of diced avocado with a toss of finely minced onion, chopped cilantro, and lime juice.

---

4 large ripe tomatoes

1 ripe avocado, peeled, pitted, and chopped

1 teaspoon freshly squeezed lime juice

Tabasco sauce

8 ounces peeled deveined cooked shrimp, roughly chopped

¼ cup Mayonnaise (page 40)

1 tablespoon minced scallion (including some of the green part)

Salt and pepper

8 Bibb lettuce leaves

4 cilantro sprigs, for garnish

---

Slice the top ½ inch off each tomato. Scoop out the seeds and pulp and place the tomatoes, cut-side down, on a double layer of paper towels to drain for at least 15 minutes.

Combine the avocado, lime juice, and Tabasco in a shallow bowl and, using a kitchen fork, mash until quite smooth.

Place the shrimp in a medium mixing bowl. Add the mashed avocado, along with the mayonnaise and scallion. Season with salt and pepper to taste and gently toss to completely blend. Stuff an equal portion of the salad into each tomato, mounding it slightly.

Place 2 lettuce leaves in the center of each of four plates. Place a tomato on the leaves, garnish with a sprig of cilantro, and serve.

*Nutritional Analysis per Serving: calories 267, carbohydrates 13 g, fiber 6 g, protein 13 g, fat 20 g, sodium 542 mg, sugar 6 g*

# Shrimp and Celery Salad

SERVES 4

This citrusy, slightly tongue-tingling dressing is a rich cover for the sweet shrimp and crisp vegetables. You can make this salad with any wild-caught meaty fish (such as halibut), free-range chicken or turkey breast, or pasture-raised organic pork.

---

½ cup Mayonnaise (page 40)

1 tablespoon freshly squeezed lime juice

1 tablespoon freshly squeezed lemon juice

2 teaspoons hot curry powder

1 pound peeled deveined cooked medium shrimp

2 celery ribs, peeled and thinly sliced on the bias

1 cup diced fennel

2 tablespoons chopped scallion

Pepper

6 cups chopped mixed salad greens

1 tablespoon snipped fresh chives, optional

---

Combine the mayonnaise with the citrus juices and curry powder in a medium mixing bowl, whisking to blend well.

Add the shrimp, celery, fennel, and scallion. Toss to lightly coat and season with pepper to taste.

Place the greens down the center of a small serving platter. Mound the salad on top. Sprinkle with chives, if desired, and serve.

**NOTE:** For those on a restricted sodium diet, the shrimp can be replaced with chunks of fresh, very rare tuna.

*Nutritional Analysis per Serving: calories 332, carbohydrates 11 g, fiber 4 g, protein 23 g, fat 24 g, sodium 884 mg, sugar 1 g*

# Niçoise Salad

Classically, a *salade niçoise* should have slices of new potatoes as a component. I've used artichoke hearts as a replacement and find that the flavor seems even more typically Provençal.

---

1 (1-pound) piece yellowfin tuna

Salt and pepper

2 tablespoons coconut oil

4 artichoke hearts (jarred, canned, or thawed frozen), quartered

2 medium beefsteak tomatoes, cored, seeded, and roughly chopped

½ cup Niçoise olives, pitted

6 cups mesclun or other mixed baby greens

⅓ cup Balsamic Vinaigrette (page 36)

4 ounces cooked haricots verts or small green or yellow beans

4 large hard-boiled eggs (see page 93), peeled and quartered

1 hunk Parmesan cheese, for shaving

---

Lightly score one side of the tuna and season with salt and pepper to taste.

Heat the oil in a medium-size heavy frying pan over high heat. When the oil is hot but not smoking, add the tuna, scored-side down. Sear for 3 minutes; then, turn and sear on the other side just until nicely colored but still almost raw in the center, about 2 minutes. Remove from the heat and place on a double layer of paper towels to drain and cool slightly.

Combine the artichoke hearts, tomatoes, and olives in a mixing bowl, stirring to mix well.

Place the greens in a large bowl. Add just enough vinaigrette to lightly coat, tossing to blend. Transfer the dressed greens to a serving platter and mound the artichoke-tomato mixture in the center.

Cut the tuna crosswise into ¼-inch-thick slices. Place the slices, slightly overlapping, around the edge of the greens. Place the haricots verts and hard-boiled eggs around the salad in an attractive pattern. Shave a few curls of Parmesan cheese over the top, drizzle the remaining vinaigrette over all, and serve.

*Nutritional Analysis per Serving: calories 442, carbohydrates 14 g, fiber 5 g, protein 36 g, fat 32 g, sodium 347 mg, sugar 4 g*

# Salmon-Avocado Salad

The sesame seeds add a hint of nuttiness to this light and extremely healthy dish, but they really wouldn't be missed if you happened to have some leftover plain grilled salmon waiting to be used. The sprouts add a nice bite; just make sure you get vegetable sprouts, not sprouts from mung beans, lentils, or wheat. If you have black sesame seeds on hand, they look splendid sprinkled on the salad just before serving.

1 (8-ounce) skinless salmon fillet

Salt and pepper

2 teaspoons sesame seeds

3 tablespoons toasted sesame oil

1 tablespoon champagne vinegar

2 cups baby arugula

1 cup green sprouts (preferably radish, but any type of vegetable sprouts can be used)

½ cup thinly sliced red radish

1 avocado, peeled, pitted, and thinly sliced

Preheat a nonstick stovetop grill pan over medium-high heat.

Season the salmon with salt and pepper to taste and then sprinkle with the sesame seeds, pressing down so they adhere to the flesh. Place the salmon in the hot pan and grill, turning once, until just barely cooked through, about 10 minutes. Remove from the heat and set aside to cool slightly.

Combine the sesame oil and vinegar in a small bowl. Season with salt and pepper to taste and whisk to blend.

Combine the arugula, sprouts, and radish in a mixing bowl. Drizzle with just enough of the sesame dressing to coat very lightly. Toss to mix well.

Place an equal portion of the dressed greens on each of two serving plates. Pull the salmon apart into chunks and place it over the greens. Garnish with avocado slices and drizzle the remaining dressing over the salmon and avocado. Serve immediately.

*Nutritional Analysis per Serving: calories 512, carbohydrates 13 g, fiber 8 g, protein 27 g, fat 42 g, sodium 686 mg, sugar 1 g*

# Kale and Bacon Frittata

SERVES 4

This egg mixture can be used with almost any combination of vegetables and/or meat. Some suggestions are broccoli-mushroom, pumpkin-mint, tomato-basil, zucchini-feta, ham-Gruyère, cheddar-bacon — the list is long and the flavors inviting.

---

5 large eggs

1½ cups finely chopped kale, Swiss chard, or spinach

¾ cup chopped cooked bacon

4 tablespoons grated Parmesan cheese

Salt and pepper

2 large egg whites

---

Preheat the oven to 350°F. Generously butter an 8-inch oven-safe frying pan and set aside.

Whisk the 5 whole eggs in a medium mixing bowl. Add the kale, bacon, and 2 tablespoons of the cheese, and season with salt and pepper to taste.

Using a hand-held electric mixer, beat the 2 egg whites until just firm but not dry. Fold the beaten egg whites into the egg mixture just until small pieces of egg white remain.

Scrape the egg mixture into the prepared pan. Sprinkle the top with the remaining 2 tablespoons cheese and transfer to the preheated oven.

Bake until the center is set and the top is golden brown and almost crisp around the edges, about 18 minutes. Remove from the oven and let stand for a couple of minutes before cutting into four wedges and serving.

*Nutritional Analysis per Serving: calories 238, carbohydrates 4 g, fiber 1 g, protein 18 g, fat 16 g, sodium 653 mg, sugar 1 g*

# Shakshuka (Eggs in Purgatory)

SERVES 4

Throughout the Middle East and Northern Africa you will find some version of this dish, but it is especially popular in Israel. It is usually quite spicy (hence the name by which it's known in English) and most often made in a cast-iron skillet. You can adjust the heat by lowering the amount of chile and red pepper flakes you use—or eliminate them altogether if you want your eggs to be more heavenly. This recipe calls for five eggs, so one lucky diner can have the bonus egg in the center of the skillet.

---

2 tablespoons extra-virgin olive oil

1 medium onion, finely diced

1 teaspoon minced garlic

1 red bell pepper, seeded and finely diced

1 hot green or red chile, seeded and minced, or to taste

4 cups tomato sauce

2 tablespoons tomato paste

1 teaspoon ground cumin

½ teaspoon red pepper flakes

Salt and pepper

5 extra-large eggs

2 tablespoons chopped fresh flat-leaf parsley

---

Preheat the oven to 350°F.

Heat the oil in a large heavy frying pan over medium heat. Add the onion and garlic and cook, stirring often, for 5 minutes. Stir in the bell pepper and chile and continue to cook, stirring frequently, until the vegetables are soft and aromatic, about 10 minutes.

Stir in the tomato sauce and tomato paste, along with the cumin and red pepper flakes. Season with salt and pepper to taste and cook, stirring frequently, just until the sauce begins to reduce slightly, about 10 minutes. (You can make the sauce and store it, covered, in the refrigerator for up to 5 days. Reheat and proceed with making the final dish. In this way, you can use only as much sauce as is needed for 1 or 2 eggs at a time, rather than all 5 at once.)

Crack one egg at a time into a small custard cup. Carefully pour out each egg into the simmering sauce in even spacing, slightly in from the edge of the pan. Place the final egg in the center.

Transfer to the preheated oven and bake just until the whites are set and the yolks still runny, about 12 minutes. Remove from the oven and sprinkle with parsley. Take the pan directly to the table and allow diners to serve themselves.

*Nutritional Analysis per Serving: calories 254, carbohydrates 25 g, fiber 6 g, protein 12 g, fat 14 g, sodium 284 mg, sugar 14 g*

# Wild Mushroom Gratin

SERVES 4

Although this gratin stands alone nicely, it also makes a terrific side dish for roast poultry or beef. If you can't find a mix of wild mushrooms, use white button mushrooms combined with cremini; the latter will add a little deeper color and flavor to the relatively bland buttons.

---

2 teaspoons unsalted butter, plus more for greasing the baking dish

1 tablespoon walnut oil

2 shallots, minced

1¾ pounds wild mushrooms, stemmed and sliced

1 teaspoon dried *fines herbes*

Salt and white pepper

2 tablespoons almond meal

½ cup heavy cream

Freshly grated nutmeg

1 cup grated Gruyère cheese

---

Preheat the oven to 350°F. Lightly butter a shallow 1-quart baking dish and set aside.

Combine the butter and oil in a large sauté pan over medium heat. Add the shallots and cook, stirring occasionally, until just translucent, about 3 minutes. Add the mushrooms and *fines herbes* and cook, stirring frequently, until the mushrooms have begun to exude their liquid and soften, about 5 minutes. Season with salt and white pepper to taste. Add the almond meal, stirring to blend, and cook for an additional couple of minutes to allow the meal to blend into the mushrooms.

Remove from the heat, stir in the cream, and season with nutmeg and, if necessary, additional salt and white pepper. Pour the mixture into the prepared baking dish and sprinkle the top with the cheese. Place in the preheated oven and bake until the edges are bubbling and the cheese is golden brown, about 12 minutes. Remove from the oven and serve.

*Nutritional Analysis per Serving: calories 359, carbohydrates 16 g, fiber 5 g, protein 16 g, fat 28 g, sodium 386 mg, sugar 4 g*

# Cheese Soufflé

SERVES 2

Most soufflés have a mixture of flour and milk to give them some binding as they rise, but this one pops right up without it. However, it does fall mighty fast, so have your forks ready as soon as it comes out of the oven. Interestingly, the nuttiness of the almond milk makes a great mate for the equally nutty Gruyère.

---

2 tablespoons grated Parmesan cheese

4 large eggs

2 ounces sour cream

2 tablespoons plus 2 teaspoons unsweetened almond milk

½ teaspoon dry mustard

Salt and pepper

1 cup (about 2 ounces) grated Gruyère cheese

---

Preheat the oven to 400°F.

Generously butter the interior of two 16-ounce ramekins. Add enough Parmesan cheese to completely coat the interior. Transfer to the refrigerator until ready to use.

Combine the eggs, sour cream, almond milk, mustard, and salt and pepper to taste in a blender, processing until very light and airy.

Remove the ramekins from the refrigerator and place half of the Gruyère in the bottom of each. Pour half of the egg mixture into each ramekin and carefully transfer to the preheated oven.

Bake until golden brown and puffed up over the edges of the ramekins, about 40 minutes. Remove from the oven and serve immediately, as the soufflés will begin falling as soon as they are out of the oven.

*Nutritional Analysis per Serving: calories 507, carbohydrates 4 g, fiber 0 g, protein 32 g, fat 40 g, sodium 672 mg, sugar 0 g*

# Falafel with Tahini Sauce

Falafel is a Middle Eastern snack or street food, usually served in a pita pocket. It is so tasty on its own that I don't think it needs anything more than a drizzle of tahini sauce to make it the perfect lunch dish, particularly if you combine it with a few tomato slices or some crunchy lettuce leaves.

Since this dish is relatively high in carbohydrates, take care about the remainder of your total carbohydrate intake for the day.

---

¾ cup dried chickpeas

1 small shallot, chopped

½ cup chopped onion

½ cup fresh cilantro leaves

1 teaspoon minced garlic

½ teaspoon ground toasted cumin

¼ teaspoon ground allspice

¼ teaspoon paprika

¼ teaspoon black pepper

¼ teaspoon cayenne pepper, or to taste

½ teaspoon baking soda

Salt

Extra-virgin olive oil, for frying

1 recipe Tahini Sauce (recipe follows)

---

Place the chickpeas in a small bowl with cold water to cover and soak for at least 8 hours or overnight.

Drain the chickpeas and rinse well under cold running water; drain again. Place in a blender and process to just chop. Add the shallot, onion, cilantro, garlic, cumin, allspice, paprika, black pepper, and cayenne and process to an almost smooth paste. If your blender isn't powerful enough to do the whole amount, process in batches to ensure a smooth mixture.

Scrape into a mixing bowl and add the baking soda and salt to taste, stirring to blend well.

Using your hands, form the mixture into 8 patties, each about 2½ inches in diameter. Don't make them too fat or the center will not cook when fried.

Heat the oil in a large frying pan (or, if you have one, a deep-fat fryer) over medium heat. It should be deep enough to cover the cakes so that they brown quickly and easily. When hot but not smoking, add the chickpea patties, a few at a time, and fry, turning once, until both sides are golden and the cakes are cooked through, about 4 minutes. Using a slotted spoon, transfer to a double layer of paper towels to drain.

Serve immediately, 2 patties per person, drizzled with 2 tablespoons tahini sauce.

*Nutritional Analysis per Serving: calories 455, carbohydrates 35 g, fiber 8 g, protein 13 g, fat 32 g, sodium 466 mg, sugar 6 g*

## *Tahini Sauce*

MAKES ABOUT ½ CUP

---

¼ cup tahini (sesame seed paste)

Juice of ½ lemon

2½ tablespoons cool water

1½ teaspoons minced fresh cilantro

½ teaspoon minced garlic

Pinch ground toasted cumin

Salt

---

Place the tahini in a small mixing bowl and gradually whisk in the lemon juice. The tahini will seize up a bit. Then, add the water, whisking until you have the consistency of creamy yogurt. Again, the mixture might seize a bit before it loosens.

Stir in the cilantro, garlic, cumin, and salt to taste. Serve immediately, or cover and store in the refrigerator for up to 5 days.

**NOTE:** Tahini sauce is outstanding on grilled fish.

*Nutritional Analysis per Serving (2 tablespoons): calories 183, carbohydrates 8 g, fiber 2 g, protein 5 g, fat 16 g, sodium 301 mg, sugar 0 g*

# Spicy Chicken Burgers with Guacamole

SERVES 4

Similar to a taco in flavor, these chicken burgers are zesty with Mexican seasonings, and the guacamole adds just the right amount of buttery smoothness to complete the package. The guacamole makes a fraction more than you will need to top the burgers, but it is so tasty that an extra helping will be appreciated. I think you'll find that you won't miss the bun one bit!

1 pound ground chicken

1 large egg white

1 jalapeño or other hot green chile, seeded and minced, or to taste

3 tablespoons minced red bell pepper

2 tablespoons minced scallion

1 teaspoon ground dried chiles, such as ancho

¼ teaspoon ground cumin

Salt and pepper

1 cup Guacamole (recipe follows)

Preheat and oil the grill; alternatively, preheat a stovetop grill pan or a heavy-bottomed frying pan over medium-high heat.

Combine the chicken with the egg white, using your hands to blend. Add the fresh chile, bell pepper, scallion, ground chiles, and cumin. Again, using your hands, mix well to blend. Season with salt and pepper to taste and form the mix into 4 patties of equal size.

Place the burgers on the preheated grill (or stovetop pan) and grill for 5 minutes. Turn and grill for another 4 minutes for well done. Remove from the grill and serve, topped with about ¼ cup guacamole.

*Nutritional Analysis per Serving: calories 309, carbohydrates 6 g, fiber 4 g, protein 29 g, fat 20 g, sodium 322 mg, sugar 1 g*

# *Guacamole*

---

2 medium avocados, peeled, pitted, and mashed

Juice of 1 lime

1/4 cup chopped tomato

2 tablespoons chopped fresh cilantro

2 tablespoons chopped scallion

1 teaspoon minced seeded jalapeño or other hot green chile,
   or to taste

Salt and pepper

---

Combine the avocado, lime juice, tomato, cilantro, scallion, and chile in a medium bowl and mix well to blend. Season with salt and pepper to taste and serve.

*Nutritional Analysis per Serving (1/4 cup): calories 86, carbohydrates 6 g, fiber 4 g, protein 1 g, fat 7 g, sodium 78 mg, sugar 1 g*

# Almond-Crusted Chicken Strips

SERVES 4 (MAKES ABOUT 12 PIECES)

This is a healthy version of those chicken fingers found in every chain restaurant. I like to dip them in a variety of sauces, but they are also delicious as is with just a sprinkle of lemon juice to cut the richness. The nut coating adds a special crunch that doesn't get soggy as a breaded coating often will. You can use pecans, walnuts, or pistachios in place of the almonds.

---

1 cup raw almonds

1 teaspoon dried Italian or pizza herb blend

¼ teaspoon smoked paprika

1 cup grated Parmesan cheese

Salt and pepper

2 large egg whites

1 pound chicken tenders

Extra-virgin olive oil, for optional drizzling

Lemon wedges, for serving

---

Preheat the oven to 375°F. Line a baking sheet with parchment paper or a nonstick silicone liner. Set aside.

Combine the almonds, herb blend, and paprika in the bowl of a food processor fitted with the metal blade. Process, using quick on and off turns, until the consistency of breadcrumbs is reached. Watch carefully, as you do not want to grind the nuts into a paste.

Combine the nut mixture with the cheese in a large shallow bowl, stirring to blend completely. Season with salt and pepper to taste.

Place the egg whites in another large shallow bowl and whisk until very light and frothy.

Working with one piece at a time, dip the chicken pieces into the egg white and then roll in the nut mixture, taking care to evenly coat all sides. Place the coated chicken on the prepared baking sheet.

When all of the chicken has been coated, lightly drizzle olive oil over each piece, if desired. Transfer to the preheated oven and bake until golden brown and cooked through, about 15 minutes. Remove from the oven and serve with lemon wedges.

*Nutritional Analysis per Serving (3 pieces): calories 501, carbohydrates 6 g, fiber 3 g, protein 43 g, fat 33 g, sodium 645 mg, sugar 1 g*

# The Best Beef 'n Cheese Burgers

SERVES 4

What, another burger? Yes, and this one has to be made with grass-fed beef, which has great omega-3 content and gives you the added strength of disease-fighting conjugated linoleic acid (see my book *Grain Brain*, pages 140–141). When you put that chunk of cheese in the center you will score a 10 on the *Grain Brain* chart. Serve with your favorite condiments, tomato slices, and lettuce leaves.

---

1 pound coarsely ground beef

¼ cup finely minced onion

2 tablespoons ice water

Salt and pepper

4 (1½-inch-long) slabs cheddar cheese

---

Place the beef in a medium bowl. Add the onion and ice water and season with salt and pepper to taste. Using your hands, gently mix to blend well.

Form the beef into 4 equal mounds. Place a slab of cheese in the center of each mound and then form the beef up and around the cheese. Shape the mounds into patties of equal size, as you want them to cook evenly.

Preheat a nonstick stovetop grill pan over medium-high heat. When very hot, add the patties and grill until crusty and nicely browned on the bottom, about 4 minutes. Turn and grill the remaining side until brown and crusty, about 4 minutes. This will result in a medium-rare burger; if you prefer it well done, give it about 4 additional minutes of cooking. Remove from the pan and serve.

*Nutritional Analysis per Serving: calories 199, carbohydrates 2 g, fiber 0 g, protein 25 g, fat 10 g, sodium 433 mg, sugar 0 g*

Manchego Tortilla (page 67)

Eggs Benedict with Zucchini Pancakes (page 60)

Thai Pork Lettuce Cups (page 96)

Tomatoes with Mozzarella, Avocado, and Basil (page 90)

Shakshuka, Eggs in Purgatory (page 108)

Salmon-Avocado Salad (page 105)

Green Beans with Walnuts (page 162)

Sautéed Cherry Tomatoes in Herbs (page 149)

Roasted Mixed Vegetables (page 127)

# Garlic-Herb Mussels

SERVES 4

Mussels are a picnic to cook and, in this recipe, the broth is as satisfying as the shellfish, so you have a two-for-one meal. Served with a tossed green salad, mussels make the perfect light lunch dish. You can add as much garlic and red pepper flakes as your palate can stand—I've gone easy here, but feel free to fire up the pot.

¼ cup extra-virgin olive oil

½ cup bottled clam juice

Juice of ½ lemon

1 tablespoon minced garlic

1 tablespoon chopped fresh basil

1 teaspoon fresh thyme leaves

Red pepper flakes

4 pounds mussels, scrubbed clean, beards removed

3 tablespoons unsalted butter, at room temperature

¼ cup chopped fresh flat-leaf parsley

Heat the oil in a large, deep sauté pan over medium heat. When hot, add the clam and lemon juices, along with the garlic, basil, thyme, and red pepper flakes to taste. Bring to a boil and immediately add the mussels. Cover and cook until all of the mussels have opened, about 6 minutes. Swirl in the butter until it melts.

Ladle the mussels and broth into four shallow soup bowls. Serve with parsley sprinkled over the top.

**VARIATIONS:** You can add 8 ounces chopped chorizo or other spicy sausage to the mussels.

*Nutritional Analysis per Serving: calories 528, carbohydrates 16 g, fiber 0 g, protein 46 g, fat 31 g, sodium 766 mg, sugar 0 g*

# DINNER

## *Vegetables, Meat, Poultry, Fish and Shellfish, and Meatless*

---

THE ONE *GRAIN BRAIN* diet caveat that many cooks find difficult is the elimination of grains and starches on the dinner plate. However, with the variety of delectable dishes in this section, I believe you will very quickly forget about potatoes, bread, and pasta. I have listed vegetable dishes first, as I encourage you to think of vegetables as the center of the plate with proteins as the accompaniment, but we do have a few non-meat main courses also. In all cases, please remember that I advocate organically grown produce; extra-virgin olive oil; organic, unsalted butter; grass-fed, pasture-raised meats; and wild, line-caught (when appropriate) fish.

## *Vegetables*

---

# Caponata

Although caponata can be eaten immediately, it is best after it rests for a day. This gives the flavors a chance to mellow and meld. It keeps very well and is terrific to have on hand for snacking or to use as a main course or in a salad. When seasoning, if you are adding capers, remember that they are going to add some salt to the mix.

---

$\frac{1}{3}$ cup extra-virgin olive oil

2 cups diced red onion

2 teaspoons minced garlic

2 pounds eggplant, cut into cubes

2 large red or green bell peppers, seeded and diced

1 (28-ounce) can diced tomatoes, with their juice

$\frac{3}{4}$ cup chopped green olives

1 tablespoon chopped fresh basil

1 teaspoon chopped fresh oregano

$\frac{3}{4}$ cup red wine vinegar

Salt and pepper

$\frac{1}{4}$ cup capers, optional

---

Heat the oil in a large nonstick frying pan over medium heat. Add the onion and garlic and cook, stirring frequently, for 5 minutes. Add the eggplant and continue to cook, stirring, just until the eggplant softens, about 20 minutes more.

Stir in the bell peppers, tomatoes, olives, basil, and oregano. Cook just until the vegetables have softened a bit, about 10 minutes. Stir in the vinegar, season with salt and pepper to taste, and bring to a boil.

Remove from the heat, stir in the capers (if using), and set aside to cool. Serve at room temperature.

**VARIATIONS:** You can add 1 large chopped zucchini with the other vegetables, and/or ½ cup pine nuts along with the capers.

*Nutritional Analysis per Serving (½ cup): calories 92, carbohydrates 10 g, fiber 2 g, protein 1 g, fat 6 g, sodium 237 mg, sugar 4 g*

# Roasted Mixed Vegetables

SERVES 6

Roasted vegetables are fantastic to have on hand—they can be eaten as is or with some shaved hard cheese for lunch or a snack, or on a platter with grilled meat or fish. They keep very well, covered and refrigerated, for up to a week. You can make as many or as few as you like and try any combination that appeals to you. You can grill these, too—the smokiness of the grill adds a whole new dimension to the flavor. You can also eliminate the vinegar if you prefer the more subtle flavor of olive oil.

2 portobello mushroom caps

2 zucchini, cut crosswise into ½-inch-thick slices

1 red bell pepper, seeded and cut lengthwise into sixths

8 ounces asparagus, tough ends removed

1 small eggplant, cut crosswise into ½-inch-thick slices

¾ cup extra-virgin olive oil

½ cup balsamic vinegar

2 teaspoons fresh rosemary

Salt and pepper

Preheat the oven to 375°F.

Place the mushrooms, zucchini, bell pepper, asparagus, and eggplant in a large baking pan. Add the olive oil, vinegar, rosemary, and salt and pepper to taste, tossing to coat well.

Place in the preheated oven and roast, turning occasionally, until the vegetables are nicely colored but still crisp-tender, about 15 minutes. Slice the mushroom caps and serve with the other vegetables.

**VARIATION:** For a southwestern flavor, replace the rosemary with 1 tablespoon chili powder, ½ teaspoon ground cumin, and ¼ teaspoon cayenne pepper.

*Nutritional Analysis per Serving: calories 298, carbohydrates 13 g, fiber 3 g, protein 3 g, fat 29 g, sodium 214 mg, sugar 8 g*

# Southwest Vegetable Sauté

SERVES 4

This vegetable stir-fry looks beautiful on the plate and makes a light dinner with a side of guacamole and Jack cheese or partnered with grilled meats or fish.

---

3 tablespoons unsalted butter

1 chayote, seeded and cut into matchsticks

1 red bell pepper, seeded and cut into matchsticks

1 carrot, peeled and cut into matchsticks

1 red onion, cut lengthwise into strips

1 small jicama, peeled and cut into matchsticks

1 teaspoon ground cumin

Salt and pepper

¼ cup chopped fresh cilantro

---

Heat the butter in a large frying pan over medium heat. Add the chayote, bell pepper, carrot, red onion, and jicama. Add the cumin and season with salt and pepper to taste. Cook, tossing and turning with tongs, just until crisp-tender, about 3 minutes.

Remove from the heat and toss in the cilantro. Serve immediately, before the hot vegetables have a chance to wilt further.

*Nutritional Analysis per Serving: calories 142, carbohydrates 15 g, fiber 6 g, protein 2 g, fat 9 g, sodium 162 mg, sugar 5 g*

# Healthy Green Slaw

SERVES 4

We usually think of slaw as a cold salad for summer barbecues and picnics. This warm slaw is quickly tossed in a wok, so the vegetables remain crisp and lively.

---

2 tablespoons avocado oil

1 small savoy cabbage, cored and cut into slivers

1 bunch kale, tough stems removed and leaves cut into slivers

Stalks from 1 bunch broccoli, peeled and cut into slivers

Salt and pepper

½ cup sunflower seeds

---

Heat the oil in a wok over medium-high heat. Add the cabbage, kale, and broccoli. Season with salt and pepper to taste and stir-fry, tossing and turning, until all of the vegetables are just barely cooked, about 5 minutes. Add the sunflower seeds, tossing to blend. Remove from the heat and serve.

*Nutritional Analysis per Serving: calories 26, carbohydrates 24 g, fiber 9 g, protein 12 g, fat 17 g, sodium 242 mg, sugar 5 g*

# Roasted Broccoli with Garlic

SERVES 4

This is one of my favorite ways to cook broccoli: a bit charred around the edges and redolent of garlic. The dish works well with almost any protein or, with a crumble of ricotta salata or a chunk of cheese melting over the top, it becomes a filling main course on its own.

---

1 bunch broccoli

2 tablespoons minced garlic

Salt

Red pepper flakes

¼ cup extra-virgin olive oil

---

Preheat the oven to 375°F.

Using a vegetable peeler, trim the outer skin from the broccoli stalks. Split each stalk, including the florets, into 2 or 3 pieces of fairly equal size. Place the stalks on a rimmed baking sheet. Sprinkle with the garlic and season with salt and red pepper flakes to taste. Pour on the olive oil and toss to evenly coat.

Transfer to the preheated oven and roast, turning occasionally, until just barely tender and slightly charred on the edges, about 15 minutes. Remove from the oven and serve hot or at room temperature.

*Nutritional Analysis per Serving: calories 221, carbohydrates 21 g, fiber 9 g, protein 7 g, fat 15 g, sodium 256 mg, sugar 4 g*

# Broccoli, Mushrooms, and Feta

SERVES 4

If you add a bit more feta to this recipe, it can stand alone on the plate. If you do, be sure to buy a beautiful imported sheep's milk feta. This recipe uses only the broccoli florets, but be sure to save the stalks. They can be peeled, cut into pieces, and sautéed or shaved into salads (or used for the Healthy Green Slaw on page 130).

2 tablespoons walnut oil

¼ cup minced shallot

8 ounces cremini mushrooms, sliced

1 bunch broccoli, cut into florets

Salt and pepper

4 ounces feta cheese, crumbled

Heat the walnut oil in a large frying pan over medium heat. Add the shallot and cook, stirring frequently, just until softened, about 2 minutes. Add the mushrooms and continue to cook, stirring frequently, just until the mushrooms have begun to exude their liquid, about 5 minutes more. Add the broccoli and season with salt and pepper to taste. Cook, tossing and turning with tongs, until the broccoli is crisp-tender, about 10 minutes.

Add the feta, cover, and remove from the heat. Let rest just until the feta begins to melt, about 2 minutes. Serve immediately.

*Nutritional Analysis per Serving: calories 259, carbohydrates 24 g, fiber 10 g, protein 13 g, fat 15 g, sodium 465 mg, sugar 6 g*

# Broccoli in Coconut Sauce

SERVES 4

This is certainly a different broccoli from the plain old green that has been so maligned over the years. The tahini and coconut add unexpected flavor and take the broccoli from the dull cafeteria table to the realm of can-I-have-seconds.

3 garlic cloves, peeled

1 hot green chile, seeded, or to taste

3 tablespoons unsweetened coconut flakes

1 tablespoon tahini

1 tablespoon extra-virgin olive oil

1 bunch broccoli, cut into florets

Salt

Preheat the oven to 350°F. Line a rimmed baking sheet with parchment paper and set aside.

Combine the garlic, chile, coconut, tahini, and olive oil in a food processor or blender and process until a smooth paste forms.

Place the broccoli in a mixing bowl, add the coconut mixture and salt to taste, and toss to coat.

Lay out the broccoli on the prepared baking sheet in a single layer. Transfer to the preheated oven and roast just until barely tender and lightly colored, about 15 minutes. Remove from the oven and serve.

*Nutritional Analysis per Serving: calories 195, carbohydrates 21 g, fiber 9 g, protein 7 g, fat 11 g, sodium 260 mg, sugar 4 g*

# Brussels Sprouts with Pancetta and Sage

SERVES 4

When I was a child no one ate Brussels sprouts; they were boiled to an unappetizing gray color and were soggy and tasteless. But they have recently gained in popularity, even in four-star restaurants, probably because nowadays they are most often roasted to bring out their inherent sweetness. Here, the salty pancetta and aromatic sage deepen the sweetness and make them particularly inviting.

---

1½ pounds Brussels sprouts, halved

8 ounces pancetta, finely diced

1 tablespoon chopped fresh sage

1 tablespoon freshly grated orange zest

2 tablespoons extra-virgin olive oil

Pepper

---

Preheat the oven to 400°F.

Combine the Brussels sprouts with the pancetta, sage, and orange zest on a rimmed baking sheet. Add the olive oil, tossing to coat well and evenly distribute all of the ingredients. Season with pepper to taste and transfer to the preheated oven. Roast, turning a couple of times, until the Brussels sprouts are tender and the pancetta is crisp, about 20 minutes. Remove from the oven and serve.

**NOTE:** For those on a restricted sodium diet, the pancetta can be eliminated from the recipe or replaced with 4 ounces low-sodium bacon.

*Nutritional Analysis per Serving: calories 348, carbohydrates 16 g, fiber 5 g, protein 13 g, fat 26 g, sodium 939 mg, sugar 3 g*

# Sautéed Greens

This is the basic method for sautéing all types of greens—collard, kale, mustard, beet, escarole, chicory, chard—well, you get it, any type of green you can find. To the basic recipe you can add a handful of pine nuts or toasted slivered almonds, a good dose of freshly grated orange or lemon zest, a chopped red or white onion, a bunch of chopped scallions, minced green or red hot chile, or any fresh herb that you favor. I make them my own by tossing in 3 tablespoons butter just before I take them off of the stove and then shaving Parmesan cheese over the top.

Please do be mindful that that huge mound of chopped raw greens will cook down to a very manageable amount, so always start with much more than you think you need—1 pound of trimmed fresh greens will yield just a little more than 1 cup cooked.

---

3 tablespoons extra-virgin olive oil

1 teaspoon minced garlic

2 bunches fresh greens, tough stems removed and leaves chopped

Salt

Red pepper flakes

¼ cup water

---

Heat the oil in a large frying pan over medium heat. Add the garlic and cook, stirring, for 2 minutes. Add the greens (they will more than fill the pan) and season with salt and red pepper flakes to taste. Add the water, cover, and cook just until the greens have wilted enough for you to be able to start tossing them, about 3 minutes.

Using tongs, toss the greens to blend the cooked ones into those that are still raw. Cover and cook until the greens are just tender, but not overcooked and soggy, about 4 minutes more. Remove from the heat and serve.

*Nutritional Analysis per Serving: calories 160, carbohydrates 13 g, fiber 3 g, protein 6 g, fat 12 g, sodium 343 mg, sugar 0 g*

# Chard Tagine

A tagine is a Moroccan stew that is often served with couscous. For a double *Grain Brain* hit, you might serve this particular stew with Cauliflower "Couscous" (page 159) for a memorable all-vegetable meal.

---

2 bunches rainbow chard, chopped

¼ cup extra-virgin olive oil

1 shallot, peeled and minced

1 cup chopped red onion

1½ teaspoons paprika

½ teaspoon ground coriander

¼ teaspoon ground cinnamon

Salt and pepper

¼ cup chopped fresh cilantro

¼ cup chopped fresh flat-leaf parsley

1 tablespoon flaxseed

1 teaspoon freshly squeezed lemon juice

---

Wash the chard well under cold running water. Place in a colander to drain, but do not dry.

Heat the oil in a large frying pan over medium heat. Add the shallot and onion, along with the paprika, coriander, and cinnamon. Cook, stirring occasionally, until the onion is very soft, about 10 minutes.

Add the reserved chard and season with salt and pepper to taste. Cover, keeping the lid askew, and cook, stirring occasionally, until the chard is tender, about 5 minutes. Remove from the heat, stir in the cilantro, parsley, flaxseed, and lemon juice, and serve.

*Nutritional Analysis per Serving: calories 256, carbohydrates 16 g, fiber 6 g, protein 6 g, fat 21 g, sodium 635 mg, sugar 5 g*

# Spinach with Scallions and Pumpkin Seeds

SERVES 4

The pumpkin seeds and scallions add a little crunch and snap to the wilted spinach. You could also use toasted pine nuts, chopped walnuts, or cashews in place of the pumpkin seeds.

---

1 pound curly-leaf spinach, tough stems removed

1 tablespoon avocado oil

Salt and cracked black pepper

¼ cup toasted pumpkin seeds

¼ cup chopped scallions (including some of the green part)

---

Wash the spinach well. Using a salad spinner, spin to dry slightly. You want to have some droplets of water clinging to the leaves.

Heat the oil in a large frying pan over medium heat. Add the spinach, season with salt and pepper to taste, and, using tongs, toss and turn to just wilt. This shouldn't take more than a minute. Toss in the pumpkin seeds and scallions and serve immediately.

*Nutritional Analysis per Serving: calories 93, carbohydrates 5 g, fiber 2 g, protein 5 g, fat 7 g, sodium 357 mg, sugar 0 g*

# Grilled Radicchio

SERVES 4

Radicchio, like all chicories, can be quite bitter, but once it is grilled the flavor mellows. Just before it is finished grilling, I often lay a couple of slices of soft cheese on the top and let it melt a bit into the radicchio, rather than shave Parmesan on after it has cooked. This dish can add a bit of pizzazz to grilled meats, poultry, or fish.

4 heads radicchio, trimmed and halved lengthwise

¼ cup extra-virgin olive oil

¼ cup balsamic vinegar

Salt and pepper

Parmesan cheese, for optional shaving

Lay the radicchio halves, cut-side up, on a rimmed baking sheet. Combine the oil and vinegar and drizzle it over the top of each piece. Set aside to marinate for 30 minutes.

Preheat and oil the grill; alternatively, oil a stovetop grill pan over high heat.

Season the radicchio with salt and pepper to taste. Place, cut-side up, on the preheated grill (or stovetop grill pan) and grill, turning occasionally, until lightly colored and cooked through, about 10 minutes.

Using tongs, transfer the radicchio to a serving platter. Let cool just a bit and then, if desired, shave Parmesan over the top and serve.

*Nutritional Analysis per Serving: calories 128, carbohydrates 2 g, fiber 0 g, protein 0 g, fat 14 g, sodium 152 mg, sugar 2 g*

# Cabbage and Onion Braise

SERVES 4

Braising the cabbage in wine softens some of the bitterness and makes a lovely flavorful broth. This is a recipe you can truly make your own by changing the spices and adding herbs and/or chiles or a touch of citrus. You don't have to add the stevia, but it does help bring out the cabbage's sweetness.

---

¼ cup unsalted butter

1 medium head green cabbage, cored and shredded

1 large onion, sliced crosswise and separated into rings

1 red bell pepper, seeded and finely diced

1 green bell pepper, seeded and cut lengthwise into strips

1 teaspoon stevia powder

1 teaspoon caraway seeds

Salt and pepper

¼ cup dry white wine

---

Preheat the oven to 350°F.

Melt the butter in a large heavy-bottomed oven-safe saucepan over medium heat. Add the cabbage, onion, and bell peppers, tossing to blend. Sprinkle on the stevia and caraway seeds and season with salt and pepper to taste. Add the white wine and again toss to blend.

Cover and transfer to the preheated oven. Cook, covered, until the vegetables are very tender and well flavored, about 30 minutes. Remove from the oven and serve.

*Nutritional Analysis per Serving: calories 171, carbohydrates 13 g, fiber 5 g, protein 3 g, fat 11 g, sodium 174 mg, sugar 6 g*

# Asparagus with Walnut Aioli

SERVES 4

Aioli is a garlic-based sauce from the Provence region of France. It is traditionally served as a sauce for steamed vegetables, fish, or hard-boiled eggs, but it can also be used as a garnish for fish stews. It can be flavored in many different ways, but this walnut version is one of my favorites. Although the recipe calls for asparagus, don't hesitate to use the sauce with other vegetables.

---

1½ pounds (about 30 spears) asparagus, trimmed of
   woody ends

1 tablespoon extra-virgin olive oil

Salt

½ cup Walnut Aioli (recipe follows)

2 tablespoons chopped toasted walnuts, optional

---

Preheat the oven to 400°F.

Lay out the asparagus on a rimmed baking sheet. Add the olive oil and salt to taste and toss to coat. Transfer to the preheated oven and roast until still slightly crisp and showing just a hint of char, about 18 minutes.

Remove from the oven and place on a serving platter. Spoon the aioli over the top, sprinkle with toasted walnuts, if desired, and serve.

*Nutritional Analysis per Serving: calories 266, carbohydrates 7 g, fiber 4 g, protein 6 g, fat 26 g, sodium 184 mg, sugar 2 g*

# Walnut Aioli

4 large egg yolks, at room temperature

2 teaspoons roasted garlic puree (see page 64)

3 tablespoons freshly squeezed lemon juice

2¾ cups extra-virgin olive oil

¼ cup walnut oil

½ cup finely chopped toasted walnuts

Salt

Cayenne pepper

Combine the egg yolks with the garlic in the bowl of a food processor fitted with the metal blade and process to blend. With the motor running, add the lemon juice through the feed tube. When the juice has blended, begin to add the olive and walnut oils in a slow, steady stream. The sauce should be quite thick and creamy.

Scrape the mixture into a clean bowl. Stir in the walnuts and season with salt and cayenne to taste. Use immediately, or cover and store in the refrigerator for up to 3 days.

*Nutritional Analysis per Serving (2 tablespoons): calories 177, carbohydrates 0 g, fiber 0 g, protein 1 g, fat 20 g, sodium 17 mg, sugar 0 g*

# Grilled Asparagus and Spring Onions

SERVES 6

This dish is perfect in the spring when both asparagus and new, almost-sweet onions are in their prime. If you can't find spring onions, look for large scallions to use in their place.

---

1 pound asparagus, trimmed of woody ends

1 pound very small spring onions or large scallions, trimmed

1 cup extra-virgin olive oil

Salt and pepper

2½ tablespoons champagne vinegar

1½ tablespoons Dijon mustard

---

Preheat and oil the grill. Alternatively, preheat the oven to 400°F.

Combine the asparagus and onions on a rimmed baking sheet (nonstick if you're planning to use the oven). Add ¼ cup of the oil, season with salt and pepper to taste, and toss to coat well.

Place the vegetables directly on the preheated grill and grill, turning frequently, until crisp-tender and nicely caramelized, about 8 minutes. If roasting, place the baking sheet in the preheated oven and roast, turning frequently, for about the same amount of time.

While the vegetables are grilling, make the dressing. Combine the vinegar and mustard in a small mixing bowl, whisking to combine. Whisk in the remaining ¾ cup olive oil, beating to emulsify. Season with salt and pepper to taste.

Remove the vegetables from the grill or oven and place on a serving platter. Drizzle the dressing over the top and serve.

*Nutritional Analysis per Serving: calories 365, carbohydrates 10 g, fiber 3 g, protein 3 g, fat 38 g, sodium 209 mg, sugar 3 g*

# Grilled Sweet and Sour Beets

SERVES 6

I guarantee that people who think they don't like beets will love this dish. There is now such a wide variety of beets available that you can make this dish into a rainbow of colors and sizes. I have seen white, candy cane, yellow, purple, Chioggia, baby, and so on. The best thing about beets is that their greens are as useful and delicious as the root, so don't discard them—you can use them to make Sautéed Greens (page 135) tomorrow.

---

¼ cup extra-virgin olive oil

¼ cup balsamic vinegar

1 tablespoon red wine vinegar

1 tablespoon stevia powder

1 teaspoon minced garlic

2 pounds cooked whole small beets or quartered large beets

Salt and pepper

---

Combine the oil with the vinegars in a large bowl, whisking to blend. Add the stevia and garlic, whisking to incorporate. Set aside, whisking occasionally, until the flavors blend.

When blended, add the beets, tossing to coat. Season with salt and pepper to taste. Set aside, tossing occasionally, for 30 minutes.

Preheat and oil the grill. Alternatively, preheat the oven to 375°F.

Place the beets on the preheated grill and grill, turning occasionally, until nicely glazed, about 5 minutes. If roasting, place the beets in a single layer on a rimmed baking sheet, place in the preheated oven, and roast until nicely glazed, about 6 minutes. Remove from the grill or oven and serve hot or at room temperature.

*Nutritional Analysis per Serving: calories 157, carbohydrates 16 g, fiber 3 g, protein 2 g, fat 9 g, sodium 154 mg, sugar 13 g*

# Radishes Braised in Butter

SERVES 4

Most Americans think of radishes used raw in a salad or as a garnish on a taco, but the French have been braising them in butter for generations. They are an inexpensive vegetable with lots of flavor, and the butter softens their piquancy so they make a tasty dish alongside almost any protein. The greens may also be used in salads or in a braise with other spicy greens; or, if you like, you can cut them into slivers and toss the raw greens with the warm radishes just before serving.

2 bunches crisp red radishes

3 tablespoons unsalted butter

⅓ cup chicken stock (page 33), low-sodium chicken broth, or water

¼ teaspoon stevia powder

Salt and pepper

Trim the radishes, leaving just a bit of the stem. Scrub them well, as dirt can often cling around the stem and root end. If they have stringy rootlets, pull off and discard.

Melt the butter over medium heat in a frying pan large enough to hold the radishes in a single layer. Add the radishes, stock, and stevia and season with salt and pepper to taste. Cover, lower the heat, and braise until easily pierced with the point of a small sharp knife, about 20 minutes. Remove from the heat and serve.

*Nutritional Analysis per Serving: calories 109, carbohydrates 7 g, fiber 3 g, protein 2 g, fat 9 g, sodium 230 mg, sugar 4 g*

# Braised Baby Artichokes

SERVES 6

Although they are not easy to find, baby artichokes are a real delicacy. Braised, they become very tender and quite unlike the large globe artichokes whose flesh has to be scraped off the leaves with your teeth. This recipe is similar to the classic Italian take on a favorite Mediterranean vegetable.

---

1 lemon

2 pounds baby artichokes

$\frac{1}{4}$ cup plus 2 tablespoons extra-virgin olive oil

2 shallots, minced

2 garlic cloves, minced

Grated zest of 1 orange

$\frac{1}{2}$ cup dry white wine

Salt and pepper

---

Fill a large bowl with cold water. Cut the lemon in half and squeeze the juice into the water. Then, add the squeezed halves.

Working with one at a time, trim the top prickly tips from each artichoke. Lay the artichoke on its side and make one swift cut with a sharp knife to neatly trim about $\frac{1}{4}$ inch off the top. If the artichoke has a stem, use a vegetable peeler to peel off the tough outer skin and lop off the dry bottom. Pull off any damaged outer leaves and then cut the artichoke in half lengthwise. Immediately place each cut artichoke into the lemon water to keep it from discoloring. Continue trimming until all of the artichokes are done.

Cover the bottom of a large sauté pan with $\frac{1}{4}$ cup of the olive oil. Place over medium heat and add the shallots and garlic. Cook, stirring frequently, just until softened, about 2 minutes.

Add the artichokes, cut-side down. Add the orange zest and white wine and season with salt and pepper to taste. Cover and bring to a simmer. Lower the heat and simmer until the artichokes are tender, about 20 minutes.

Remove from the heat and drizzle with the remaining 2 tablespoons olive oil. Taste and, if necessary, season with additional salt and pepper. Serve warm or at room temperature. Or, cool, cover, and store in the refrigerator for up to 1 week. Bring to room temperature before serving.

*Nutritional Analysis per Serving: calories 117, carbohydrates 10 g, fiber 4 g, protein 2 g, fat 7 g, sodium 155 mg, sugar 2 g*

# Grilled Parmesan Tomatoes

SERVES 4

One tomato is usually enough for a serving, but these are so tasty I suggest you make a couple of extras—if not eaten, they can be served at room temperature for lunch tomorrow. The tomatoes can also be cooked entirely under a preheated broiler, but do watch carefully to keep the cheese from burning.

---

4 large ripe but firm tomatoes

6 tablespoons grated Parmesan cheese

1 tablespoon chopped fresh basil

2 tablespoons unsalted butter, melted

Salt and pepper

---

Preheat and oil the grill or preheat the oven to 375°F.

Cut each tomato in half crosswise.

Combine the cheese and basil in a small bowl. Spoon equal portions of the mixture on the cut side of each tomato half. Drizzle with melted butter and season with salt and pepper to taste.

Place the tomatoes, cut-side up, on the preheated grill. Cover and grill for 3 minutes. Uncover and grill until the top is bubbling, another minute or so. Alternatively, place the tomatoes on a rimmed baking sheet in the preheated oven and bake until the top is bubbling, about 10 minutes. (If you want the tops to brown, preheat the broiler and place the grilled tomatoes under the broiler for 30 seconds or so.)

Remove from the grill or oven and serve.

*Nutritional Analysis per Serving: calories 131, carbohydrates 9 g, fiber 2 g, protein 5 g, fat 9 g, sodium 341 mg, sugar 5 g*

# Sautéed Cherry Tomatoes in Herbs

SERVES 4

This dish is lovely when done with cherry tomatoes of different sizes and colors. Even if they are tiny, cut them in half—otherwise you'll get a good squirt of juice in the eye when you prick them with your fork. To change the flavor, substitute extra-virgin olive oil for the butter.

---

⅓ cup unsalted butter

2 pints mixed cherry tomatoes, halved

Salt and pepper

2 tablespoons chopped fresh flat-leaf parsley

2 tablespoons chopped fresh chives

2 tablespoons chopped fresh basil

---

Heat the butter in a large frying pan over medium heat. Add the tomatoes, season with salt and pepper to taste, and cook, stirring occasionally, until just barely soft and oozing their juices, about 4 minutes. Do not overcook or you will have mush.

Remove from the heat and stir in the parsley, chives, and basil. Taste and, if necessary, add additional salt. Serve warm or at room temperature.

*Nutritional Analysis per Serving: calories 162, carbohydrates 6 g, fiber 2 g, protein 2 g, fat 15 g, sodium 299 mg, sugar 4 g*

# Fried Green Plantains (*Tostones*)

SERVES 4

Plantains are not often found on most American tables, except on those of families from Caribbean or Latin American countries, where they are an everyday staple. One of the most popular ways to cook plantains is to fry them until crisp and golden. *Tostones* also make an unsurpassed snack. You can substitute extra-virgin olive oil or avocado oil for the coconut oil.

---

Coconut oil

2 green plantains

Salt

---

Place about 3 inches of oil in a medium saucepan over medium-high heat. Bring to 375°F on a candy thermometer.

While the oil is heating, peel the plantains and cut them crosswise into ¾-inch-thick slices.

When the oil has reached temperature, begin frying the plantains. Do not crowd the pan. Fry until just tender, about 3 minutes. Do not turn off the heat; maintain the temperature.

Use a slotted spoon to lift the plantains from the oil and place on a double layer of paper towels to drain for 1 minute.

Using a large fork, smash the warm slices into flattened rounds. Return to the hot oil, in batches, and fry until very crisp and golden brown, about 4 minutes. Continue frying until all of the plantains are done, transferring them back to the paper towels as they finish.

Generously sprinkle with salt and serve while still hot and crisp.

*Nutritional Analysis per Serving: calories 229, carbohydrates 29 g, fiber 2 g, protein 1 g, fat 13 g, sodium 294 mg, sugar 13 g*

# Butternut Squash with Spinach and Pistachios

SERVES 4

You can make this dish with any type of hard winter squash, including pump-kin. If you want to make it a main course, add about 8 ounces crumbled ricotta salata or feta cheese when the squash is still hot. The cheese will melt a bit and add some brininess to the sweet roasted squash.

---

2 pounds butternut squash, peeled, seeded, and cut into large cubes (see Note)

3 tablespoons clarified butter (see page 42), ghee, or unsalted butter, melted

2 tablespoons balsamic vinegar

1 teaspoon freshly squeezed lemon juice

Salt and pepper

3 cups baby spinach or arugula or finely chopped greens of choice

½ cup toasted unsalted pistachios

---

Preheat the oven to 350°F. Line a rimmed baking sheet with parchment paper and set aside.

Combine the squash with the clarified butter, vinegar, and lemon juice in a large mixing bowl. Season with salt and pepper to taste and toss to coat well.

Spread the seasoned squash in a single layer on the prepared baking sheet. Transfer to the preheated oven and roast, turning occasionally, until golden brown and tender, about 25 minutes.

Place the spinach in a large mixing bowl. Remove the squash from the oven and add it to the spinach. Add the nuts and toss to blend. Taste and, if necessary, season with additional salt and pepper. Serve immediately.

**NOTE:** Make sure that the squash cubes are of an equal size so that they roast evenly.

*Nutritional Analysis per Serving: calories 248, carbohydrates 27 g, fiber 9 g, protein 5 g, fat 15 g, sodium 499 mg, sugar 6 g*

# Zucchini Casserole with Prosciutto and Cheese

SERVES 4

This dish partners well with grilled meat or poultry since it is quite rich, but it can certainly stand alone as a filling lunch or brunch dish, or even as a light supper.

---

2 tablespoons extra-virgin olive oil

2 tablespoons unsalted butter

1½ pounds zucchini, cut crosswise into ¼-inch-thick slices

4 large eggs

½ cup chopped prosciutto

¼ cup chopped sun-dried tomatoes

¼ cup grated Asiago or Parmesan cheese

Pepper

---

Preheat the oven to 400°F.

Heat the oil and butter in a large cast-iron skillet over medium heat. Add the zucchini and cook, stirring frequently, just until they begin to soften and exude their liquid, about 5 minutes. Remove from the heat.

Beat the eggs in a large mixing bowl. Stir in the prosciutto, sun-dried tomatoes, and cheese and season with pepper to taste. Pour the egg mixture over the zucchini. Transfer to the preheated oven and bake until the center is set and the top is golden brown, about 20 minutes. Remove from the oven, cut into quarters, and serve.

*Nutritional Analysis per Serving: calories 294, carbohydrates 9 g, fiber 2 g, protein 17 g, fat 22 g, sodium 712 mg, sugar 5 g*

# Celery and Fennel with Anchovy Sauce

SERVES 4

This dish is unusual in its flavor and in the combination of celery and fennel, two vegetables we usually eat raw. Don't forget to save some of the fennel fronds for garnish — they add a wonderful freshness to the warm vegetables.

---

½ cup chicken stock (page 33) or low-sodium chicken broth

2 garlic cloves, peeled

1 bay leaf

¼ teaspoon coriander seeds

¼ teaspoon fennel seeds

2 anchovy fillets, drained and chopped

1 tablespoon extra-virgin olive oil

1 tablespoon chopped fresh flat-leaf parsley

1 teaspoon chopped capers

1 teaspoon freshly grated orange zest

½ teaspoon red wine vinegar

Pepper

5 celery ribs, peeled and cut on the bias into ¼-inch-thick slices

2 fennel bulbs, quartered lengthwise and cut on the bias into ¼-inch-thick slices

Fennel fronds, for optional garnish

---

Place the chicken stock in a small saucepan over medium heat. Add the garlic, bay leaf, coriander, and fennel seeds and bring to a simmer. Cover and simmer until the stock is well flavored, about 10 minutes. Strain the broth through a fine-mesh sieve into a large, shallow saucepan or deep frying pan and set aside. Reserve the garlic but discard the bay leaf and seeds.

Combine the garlic, anchovies, and oil in a small bowl. Use a fork to mash the mixture together until quite smooth. Stir in the parsley, capers, orange zest, and vinegar. Season with pepper to taste and set aside.

Heat the reserved seasoned chicken stock over medium heat. Add the celery and fennel, cover, and bring to a simmer. Simmer, covered, until barely tender, about 4 minutes.

Remove from the heat and drain well. Transfer to a warm serving bowl, add the reserved anchovy sauce, season with pepper to taste, and toss to coat. Cover and let marinate for 1 minute. Uncover and serve, garnished with fennel fronds, if desired.

*Nutritional Analysis per Serving: calories 85, carbohydrates 11 g, fiber 5 g, protein 3 g, fat 4 g, sodium 340 mg, sugar 1 g*

# Kohlrabi Gratin

SERVES 6

Kohlrabi is one of the most underused vegetables, probably because it looks weird and few cooks know what to do with it. In Southeast Asia, it is as popular as carrots are in the United States. Kohlrabi must be thoroughly peeled before being cooked—first off is the outer layer of skin, and then a second fibrous layer has to go. So when buying kohlrabi, purchase more than you think you need because you are going to lose much of it as you peel. This is another vegetable whose greens can be eaten, but they are rarely attached unless bought straight from the farm; they might be green or a beautiful purplish-pink.

---

1¼ cups unsweetened almond milk

2 garlic cloves, halved

2 bay leaves

2 thyme sprigs

½ teaspoon freshly grated nutmeg

4 pounds kohlrabi, peeled (see headnote) and cut crosswise into ⅛-inch-thick slices

¾ cup grated Parmesan cheese

Salt and white pepper

¼ cup chopped raw almonds

---

Preheat the oven to 400°F. Generously butter a 2-quart casserole and set aside.

Combine the almond milk, garlic, bay leaves, thyme, and nutmeg in a small saucepan over medium heat. Bring to a simmer and immediately remove from the heat.

Place the kohlrabi in a large mixing bowl. Pour the hot milk over the kohlrabi through a fine-mesh strainer, discarding the solids. Add ½ cup of the cheese, season with salt and white pepper to taste, and toss to coat.

Using your hands, layer the kohlrabi slices in the casserole, taking care that they are evenly spaced. Pour any remaining milk over the kohlrabi and sprinkle the remaining ¼ cup cheese over the top. Cover with aluminum foil and transfer to the preheated oven. Bake for 30 minutes. Uncover, sprinkle the almonds over the top, and continue to bake until the top is golden brown and the kohlrabi is cooked through, about 15 minutes more. Remove from the oven and serve.

*Nutritional Analysis per Serving: calories 237, carbohydrates 23 g, fiber 5 g, protein 13 g, fat 11 g, sodium 438 mg, sugar 9 g*

# Cauliflower with Lemon-Parsley Butter

SERVES 4

A wonderfully fragrant sauce accents the sweetness of the roasted cauliflower in this recipe. The nutty crunch of the sunflower seeds adds that over-the-top extra dimension. This dish can also be served as a warm salad with the addition of chunks of cheese and/or chopped bitter greens.

---

1 head white, yellow, or purple cauliflower or broccoflower

¼ cup clarified butter (see page 42), ghee, or unsalted butter, melted

Salt and pepper

Juice and grated zest of 1 lemon

1 cup fresh flat-leaf parsley leaves

2 tablespoons extra-virgin olive oil

½ cup sunflower seeds

---

Preheat the oven to 425°F.

Cut the cauliflower into florets and place in a mixing bowl. Add the clarified butter, season with salt and pepper to taste, and toss to coat. Transfer to a rimmed baking sheet and place in the preheated oven. Roast, turning occasionally, until tender and slightly charred, about 25 minutes.

While the cauliflower is roasting, prepare the sauce. Place the lemon juice and zest, parsley, and olive oil in the bowl of a food processor fitted with the metal blade and process until almost a puree. Season with salt and pepper to taste.

Remove the cauliflower from the oven and pour the sauce over the top. Add the sunflower seeds and toss to coat. Serve hot or at room temperature.

*Nutritional Analysis per Serving: calories 335, carbohydrates 12 g, fiber 6 g, protein 7 g, fat 31 g, sodium 180 mg, sugar 4 g*

# Cauliflower "Couscous"

SERVES 4

With so much interest in plant-based diets, cooks have come up with all kinds of inventive methods for cooking vegetables. Turning cauliflower into little couscous-like nuggets is one of the winners. Steamed, it can become a base for stews and sauces; it can also be seasoned in any number of ways to make a terrific side dish. I will give you a couple of ideas of things to do with this vegetable "couscous," but I urge you to use your imagination to take it all over the world with the addition of other vegetables, spices, sauces, and/or herbs.

---

1 head cauliflower (see Note)

---

Cut the cauliflower into pieces and place them in the bowl of a food processor fitted with the metal blade. Process using quick on and off turns until the cauliflower looks like tiny little nuggets. Watch carefully, as it doesn't take long to turn nuggets into puree. If you don't have a food processor, you can either grate the cauliflower on the large holes of a box grater or chop it using a very sharp chef's knife.

**VARIATIONS:** Here is where the fun begins.

You can line a steamer basket with cheesecloth and set it in a large stockpot with just enough water to come up to the bottom of the steamer basket. Bring the water to a boil over high heat. Place the cauliflower nuggets in the steamer basket and season with salt to taste. Cover and steam just until the cauliflower is barely cooked, about 4 minutes. Again, don't turn it into mush. This gives you a plain couscous-like base for sauces or stews.

Or, you can heat about 2 tablespoons extra-virgin olive oil in a large frying pan. Add 1 finely diced onion and 1 teaspoon minced garlic and cook, stirring, just until soft, about 3 minutes. Add the raw cauliflower nuggets, season with salt and pepper to taste, and cook, stirring, until the cauliflower begins to color, about 5 minutes. Remove from the heat and stir in 1 tablespoon minced fresh herbs of choice, chopped scallions, chopped olives or sun-dried tomatoes, orange zest, or pomegranate seeds and serve as a side dish. Or, when sautéing the onion and garlic, you can add chopped nuts or pine nuts, diced celery, a couple of handfuls of chopped bitter greens, or anything you like that might work with the protein or stew you are serving it with.

**NOTE:** Many people discard the core of the cauliflower and use only the florets to make "couscous." I have found that there is absolutely no sound reason for doing this—the core tastes only a bit stronger than the florets and adds at least one more serving to the mix.

*Nutritional Analysis per Serving (1 cup): calories 38, carbohydrates 7 g, fiber 4 g, protein 3 g, fat 1 g, sodium 170 mg, sugar 3 g*

# Sesame-Scented Green and Yellow Beans

SERVES 4

The mix of green and yellow accented with the black sesame seeds creates a beautiful side dish for almost any protein. If you can't find black sesame seeds, toast some white ones to a nice golden brown.

---

8 ounces green beans, trimmed

8 ounces yellow wax beans, trimmed

1 tablespoon toasted sesame oil

2 teaspoons unsalted butter, melted

1 tablespoon black sesame seeds

Salt and pepper

---

Set a steamer basket in a large saucepan with just enough water to come up to the bottom of the steamer basket. Bring the water to a boil over high heat. Place the beans in the steamer basket, cover, and steam until crisp-tender, about 5 minutes.

Remove from the steamer and pat dry. Place on a serving plate and add the sesame oil, butter, and sesame seeds, tossing to coat well. Season with salt and pepper to taste and serve hot or at room temperature.

*Nutritional Analysis per Serving: calories 91, carbohydrates 7 g, fiber 3 g, protein 2 g, fat 7 g, sodium 152 mg, sugar 3 g*

# Green Beans with Walnuts

These beans are a perfect match with almost any meat or fish. The walnuts add an unusual dimension so that everyday green beans become the star of the plate.

---

1 pound green beans, trimmed and cut crosswise into 2-inch pieces

3 tablespoons unsalted butter

⅓ cup chopped raw walnuts

1 teaspoon freshly grated orange zest

Salt and pepper

---

Place the beans in a large stockpot and cover with cold water. Bring to a boil over high heat and then immediately lower the heat to a simmer. Simmer until crisp-tender, about 4 minutes. Remove from the heat and drain well. Pat dry.

Heat the butter in a medium frying pan over medium heat. Add the walnuts and cook, stirring constantly, just until the nuts begin to color, about 2 minutes. Add the beans and, using tongs, toss and turn to coat well. Add the orange zest and season with salt and pepper to taste. Transfer to a large bowl and serve.

*Nutritional Analysis per Serving: calories 171, carbohydrates 8 g, fiber 4 g, protein 4 g, fat 15 g, sodium 151 mg, sugar 3 g*

# Meat

_____

# Roast Tenderloin of Beef Wrapped in Bacon

SERVES 6

This is the ultimate dinner party or buffet dish. It can be served hot or at room temperature, and the smoky, fatty bacon is the perfect foil for the tender, mildly flavored meat. A lovely platter of mixed roasted vegetables (page 127) would make the meal complete—they, too, can be served hot or at room temperature.

1 (1½-pound) tenderloin of beef, trimmed of all fat and silverskin

Cracked black pepper

1 pound thick-sliced bacon

Preheat the oven to 450°F.

Season the tenderloin generously with cracked black pepper.

Lay out the bacon slices, slightly overlapping, on a clean work surface. When finished you should have a rectangle large enough to cover the beef. Lay the tenderloin in the center of the bacon rectangle and then pull the bacon up on both sides to completely cover the meat. Using kitchen twine, tie the bacon in place around the meat by wrapping the twine around the meat in sections about 2 inches apart.

Place the bacon-wrapped tenderloin in the center of a small roasting pan in the preheated oven. Roast until an instant-read thermometer inserted into the center reads 125°F for rare or 140°F for medium-rare, about 25 minutes.

Remove from the oven and allow to rest for 10 minutes. Cut the twine and discard it. Then cut the bacon-wrapped meat crosswise into ½-inch-thick slices and serve.

*Nutritional Analysis per Serving: calories 280, carbohydrates 0 g, fiber 0 g, protein 31 g, fat 15 g, sodium 695 mg, sugar 0 g*

# Steak Diane

SERVES 4

This classic, old-time restaurant dish is easily made at home. The most important thing to remember is that the steaks cook very quickly, and since they are low in fat, if you overcook them they will be dry and tough.

---

4 (6-ounce) filet mignon steaks

Salt and pepper

4 tablespoons unsalted butter

2 tablespoons extra-virgin olive oil

3 tablespoons minced shallot

1 tablespoon cognac

4 tablespoons chopped fresh flat-leaf parsley

2 teaspoons beef stock (page 33) or low-sodium beef broth

1 teaspoon Dijon mustard

½ teaspoon Worcestershire sauce

---

Place the steaks on a clean, flat work surface and, using a meat mallet, pound until approximately ½ inch thick. Season with salt and pepper to taste.

Heat 2 tablespoons of the butter with the olive oil in a large frying pan over medium-high heat. When very hot but not smoking, add the steaks. Fry for about 90 seconds and then turn and fry for another 30 seconds. Do not overcook; the meat should be very rare as it will continue to cook while it sits, and the hot sauce will cook it further. Remove the pan from the heat and transfer the steaks to a warm serving platter.

Add the shallot to the pan and return it to medium heat. Stir to blend the shallot into the pan juices and then add the cognac, swirling the pan to combine. Stir in 3 tablespoons of the parsley, along with the stock, mustard, and Worcestershire sauce. When blended, stir in the remaining 2 tablespoons butter. When the butter has melted into the pan sauce, taste and, if necessary, season with salt and pepper to taste.

Pour the sauce over the steaks, sprinkle with the remaining 1 tablespoon parsley, and serve immediately.

*Nutritional Analysis per Serving: calories 425, carbohydrates 2 g, fiber 0 g, protein 33 g, fat 31 g, sodium 401 mg, sugar 1 g*

# Filet Mignon with Compound Butter

SERVES 4

Although filet mignon is extremely tender, because it is low in fat it is not as richly flavored as many other steaks. The melting butter adds just that extra ounce of fat and flavor needed to heighten the beefiness of the filet. Compound butters are easy to make and a boon to keep on hand as they add elegant flavor to all types of grilled meats, poultry, and even fish. The following recipe should yield enough to season quite a few dishes.

---

4 (5-ounce) filet mignon steaks

1 tablespoon extra-virgin olive oil

Salt and pepper

4 tablespoons Compound Butter (recipe follows)

---

Rub the steaks on all sides with the oil and then season with salt and pepper to taste.

Place a heavy-bottomed frying pan over high heat. When very hot, add the seasoned steaks and fry, turning occasionally, for about 9 minutes for rare (125°F on an instant-read thermometer), or until they reach the desired degree of doneness.

Remove from the pan and allow to rest for 2 minutes. Place 1 tablespoon compound butter on the top of each hot steak, allowing it to melt slightly before serving.

*Nutritional Analysis per Serving: calories 346, carbohydrates 1 g, fiber 0 g, protein 27 g, fat 25 g, sodium 285 mg, sugar 0 g*

# Compound Butter

---

1 cup unsalted butter, at room temperature

1 shallot, minced

1 tablespoon chopped fresh flat-leaf parsley

1 teaspoon freshly squeezed lemon juice

Salt and pepper

---

Combine the butter, shallot, parsley, and lemon juice in the bowl of a food processor fitted with the metal blade and process to thoroughly blend.

Using a rubber spatula, scrape the butter into the center of a piece of plastic wrap or waxed paper. Fold the wrap over the butter and form the butter into a neat log about $1\frac{1}{2}$ inches in diameter. Tightly close the ends of the plastic wrap and transfer the log to the refrigerator. Chill until firm, at least 1 hour, or freeze for up to 3 months.

When ready to use, unwrap the log and cut the butter crosswise into $\frac{1}{4}$-inch-thick slices. Bring to room temperature before serving.

**NOTE:** Other herbs may replace or be combined with the parsley. Tarragon, marjoram, and basil are particularly good choices.

*Nutritional Analysis per Serving: calories 102, carbohydrates 1 g, fiber 0 g, protein 0 g, fat 11 g, sodium 37 mg, sugar 0 g*

# London Broil with Grilled Mushrooms

SERVES 4

This recipe can be made with almost any steak or chop except filet mignon, which is too tender to take a long marination. The steak-mushroom combination also makes a fantastic salad either placed on top of or tossed with arugula and tomatoes—or, in fact, almost any other vegetable you like.

An outdoor grill adds lovely flavor to this, but if you don't have one, a stovetop grill pan is the next best alternative. They are inexpensive and easy to use, with the resulting char resembling grilled meat.

---

1 (1¼-pound) round steak (about 1½ inches thick)

¾ cup extra-virgin olive oil

¼ cup balsamic vinegar

1 teaspoon freshly grated orange zest

4 tablespoons chopped fresh flat-leaf parsley

Salt and pepper

4 large portobello mushroom caps

---

Place the steak in a large resealable plastic bag along with the oil, vinegar, orange zest, and 1 tablespoon of the parsley. Seal and push the steak around to coat well. Refrigerate for at least 1 hour but no more than 3 hours.

When ready to grill, remove the meat from the refrigerator and bring to room temperature. Preheat and oil the grill; alternatively, preheat a stovetop grill pan over medium-high heat.

Remove the steak from the plastic bag and season with salt and pepper to taste.

Place the mushroom caps in the plastic bag, seal, and push them around to coat. Remove the mushrooms from the bag and season with salt and pepper to taste.

Place the steak and the mushrooms, caps down, on the preheated grill (or stovetop grill pan) and grill for 10 minutes.

Turn the steak and grill for another 10 minutes for medium-rare, or until it reaches the desired degree of doneness on an instant-read thermometer. At the same time, turn the mushrooms and move them to the outer edge of the grill. Grill until just beginning to char, about 8 minutes more. Remove from the grill. Remove the steak from the grill and set aside for 5 minutes.

Cut the steak and mushrooms into strips and place on a platter. Sprinkle with the remaining 3 tablespoons parsley and serve.

*Nutritional Analysis per Serving: calories 345, carbohydrates 6 g, fiber 2 g, protein 33 g, fat 21 g, sodium 345 mg, sugar 4 g*

# Grilled Spiced Flank Steak

SERVES 6

You can make this as hot and spicy as you wish. Mixed peppercorns, available at most supermarkets, are somewhat milder than straight black peppercorns. This sliced steak is terrific as a salad topper or served with an assortment of grilled vegetables.

---

2 tablespoons mixed or all-black cracked peppercorns

½ teaspoon cayenne pepper, or to taste

½ teaspoon hot paprika

½ teaspoon garlic salt

Salt

1 (2-pound) beef or veal flank steak

---

Preheat and oil the grill; alternatively, preheat a stovetop grill pan over medium-high heat.

Combine the cracked pepper with the cayenne, paprika, garlic salt, and salt to taste in a small bowl. Generously coat both sides of the steak with the pepper mix.

Place on the preheated grill (or stovetop grill pan) and grill for 6 minutes. Turn and grill for an additional 7 minutes for medium-rare, or until it reaches the desired degree of doneness on an instant-read thermometer.

Remove the steak from the grill and place on a cutting board to rest for 3 minutes. Cut on the bias into thin slices and serve.

*Nutritional Analysis per Serving: calories 234, carbohydrates 2 g, fiber 1 g, protein 31 g, fat 11 g, sodium 189 mg, sugar 0 g*

# Southwest-Style Rib-Eye Steaks

SERVES 4

Rib-eye steaks can be either boneless or bone-in; I prefer the latter. A first-class rib-eye is well marbled with fat and quite tender. Although grass-fed beef is more readily available, a buffalo rib-eye is equally delicious if you can find it. The green chile sauce is mild and can be used on any meat or poultry to add a hint of zestiness. It keeps, tightly covered and refrigerated, for up to 2 weeks.

---

1 pound fresh mild green chiles, such as Anaheim

2 tablespoons coconut oil

1 cup chopped onion

1 teaspoon minced garlic

1 cup beef stock (page 33) or low-sodium beef broth

Salt and pepper

4 (12-ounce) rib-eye steaks (about 1½ inches thick)

2 tablespoons ground dried chiles, such as ancho

---

Preheat the oven to 450°F.

Place the fresh chiles on a nonstick baking pan and roast until well charred, about 20 minutes. Remove from the oven and allow to cool.

When the chiles are cool enough to handle, peel, stem, and seed them.

Heat the oil in a medium saucepan over medium heat. Add the onion and garlic and sauté for 3 minutes. Add the reserved chiles, along with the beef stock and salt and pepper to taste. Bring to a simmer and simmer until quite thick, about 20 minutes.

Transfer the sauce to a blender. Holding down the lid with a kitchen towel (to keep the heat from pushing it off), process until smooth. Transfer to a serving bowl to pass when you serve the steaks.

Preheat and oil the grill; alternatively, preheat a stovetop grill pan or cast-iron skillet over medium-high heat.

Season both sides of the steaks with the ground chiles and salt and pepper to taste. Place on the preheated grill (or stovetop grill pan) and grill for 10 minutes. Turn the steak and grill for 12 additional minutes for medium-rare (135°F on an instant-read thermometer), or until cooked to the desired degree of doneness.

Remove from the grill and serve with the sauce on the side.

*Nutritional Analysis per Serving: calories 754, carbohydrates 14 g, fiber 3 g, protein 79 g, fat 42 g, sodium 396 mg, sugar 7 g*

# Braised Beef Brisket

SERVES 6

You cannot imagine a more flavorful "pot roast" than this brisket. The onions seep into the meat during the slow braise and melt into the most delicious gravy you can imagine.

---

1 (2½-pound) beef brisket

Salt and pepper

2 tablespoons avocado oil

6 large onions, cut crosswise into thin slices

1 tablespoon minced garlic

---

Season the meat with salt and pepper to taste.

Heat the oil in a Dutch oven over medium heat. Add the seasoned meat and sear, turning frequently, until nicely browned, about 5 minutes.

Transfer the meat to a plate. Lay the onions and garlic in the bottom of the pan. Place the meat on top of the onions, cover, and cook until the meat is fork tender and the onions have melted into a gravy, about 2 hours. After about 1 hour, you can lower the heat, but keep the pan covered or the liquid from the onions will evaporate.

Using tongs, transfer the meat to a cutting board. Cut the meat across the grain into thin slices. Place on a serving platter and spoon the onion gravy over the top. Serve immediately.

*Nutritional Analysis per Serving: calories 303, carbohydrates 15 g, fiber 3 g, protein 34 g, fat 11 g, sodium 445 mg, sugar 6 g*

# Meatloaf Stuffed with Hard-Boiled Eggs

SERVES 6

I do wonder what prompted the first cook to place hard-boiled eggs down the center of a meatloaf, but perhaps those many years ago she was already aware of the *Grain Brain* regimen. I say "she" because I am pretty sure it was a home cook and mom in the 1930s who came up with a version of this recipe to feed her hungry family.

---

12 ounces ground beef

12 ounces ground pork

1 cup finely chopped onion

1 cup grated Parmesan cheese

1 tablespoon finely chopped fresh basil

1 teaspoon finely chopped fresh oregano

1 teaspoon minced garlic

1 large egg, beaten

Salt and pepper

3 large hard-boiled eggs (see page 93), peeled

$\frac{1}{2}$ cup beef stock (page 33) or low-sodium beef broth

$\frac{1}{2}$ cup diced canned or fresh tomatoes, with their juice

1 tablespoon extra-virgin olive oil

---

Preheat the oven to 375°F.

Combine the beef and pork with the onion, grated cheese, basil, oregano, and garlic, using your hands to mix. Add the raw egg, season with salt and pepper to taste, and continue to mix with your hands until completely blended.

Place half of the meat mixture in the center of a baking dish, forming it into a neat rectangle approximately 4 inches wide. Arrange the hard-boiled eggs down the center of the rectangle. Place the remaining meat over the top of the eggs and, using your hands, enclose the eggs as you form the meat into a neat, seamless rectangle.

Combine the beef stock and tomatoes in a small mixing bowl. Season with salt and pepper to taste.

Using a pastry brush, generously coat the exterior of the meatloaf with oil. Pour the beef stock mixture into the pan and transfer to the preheated oven.

Bake, occasionally basting with the pan liquid, until an instant-read thermometer inserted into the thickest part registers 155°F, about 45 minutes.

Remove from the oven and let rest for about 10 minutes before cutting crosswise into thick slices. Place on a serving platter and spoon any remaining pan juices over the meat. Serve hot or at room temperature.

*Nutritional Analysis per Serving: calories 376, carbohydrates 4 g, fiber 1 g, protein 34 g, fat 23 g, sodium 633 mg, sugar 2 g*

# Traditional Chophouse Mixed Grill

SERVES 4

A mixed grill has been a traditional lunch in men's clubs for generations but is rarely found on menus today. It can have kidneys and sausages added to the mix as well as the meats I use in this recipe. It is often served with a bowl of grainy mustard and some sour pickles. If you don't have an outdoor grill, a stovetop grill pan can be used, but you will most likely have to cook the various ingredients in batches.

---

2 tomatoes, cored and halved crosswise

⅓ cup clarified butter (see page 42), ghee, or unsalted butter, melted

Salt and pepper

2 tablespoons grated Parmesan cheese

2 red onions, halved crosswise

4 large button mushroom caps

1 (1-pound) sirloin steak

2 small slices calf's liver (about 5 ounces total), halved

4 (3-ounce) lamb rib chops

4 thick slices slab bacon or pork belly (about 3 ounces total)

---

Preheat and oil the grill; alternatively, preheat a stovetop grill pan over medium-high heat.

Using a pastry brush, lightly coat the cut side of each tomato half with clarified butter. Season with salt and pepper to taste and sprinkle with the grated cheese. Set aside.

Run a metal skewer crosswise through each onion half to help it hold its shape when grilling. Using a pastry brush, lightly coat the cut side of each half with clarified butter and season with salt and pepper to taste. Set aside.

Using a pastry brush, lightly coat the mushrooms with clarified butter and season with salt and pepper to taste. Set aside.

Rub the steak, liver, and lamb chops with clarified butter and season with salt and pepper to taste.

Place the steak in the center of the grill, cover, and grill for 10 minutes. Uncover, turn the steak, and place the liver, lamb chops, bacon, tomatoes, onions, and mushrooms on the grill, with the lamb nearest the hotter center. Cover and grill, turning the liver, lamb, bacon, and onion once, for another 10 minutes, for the steak to reach medium-rare and the lamb medium, or until they reach the desired degree of doneness on an instant-read thermometer. At about 6 minutes begin checking the liver, bacon, and vegetables as you don't want them to overcook. (If using a stovetop grill pan, everything will have to be done in batches.)

Remove all of the meats and vegetables from the grill. Remove the skewers from the onions.

Cut the steak into slices and place an equal portion on each of four dinner plates. Place a lamb chop, a slice each of liver and bacon, an onion half, a tomato half, and a mushroom on each plate and serve.

*Nutritional Analysis per Serving: calories 502, carbohydrates 11 g, fiber 2 g, protein 41 g, fat 32 g, sodium 480 mg, sugar 5 g*

# Tex-Mex Cowboy Burgers with Tomato-Onion Salsa

SERVES 4

A little Tex-Mex twist to the classic burger elevates it up and away from the bun and fries. You can make both the burgers and the salsa as hot or as mild as you wish by adjusting the amount of fresh chiles you add.

---

8 ounces ground sirloin

8 ounces ground pork

3 tablespoons finely chopped red bell pepper

2 tablespoons finely chopped red onion

2 teaspoons ground dried chiles, such as ancho

½ teaspoon ground cumin

Salt and pepper

1 cup Tomato-Onion Salsa (recipe follows)

---

Preheat and oil the grill; alternatively, preheat a stovetop grill pan or a cast-iron frying pan over medium-high heat.

Combine the sirloin and pork with the bell pepper, onion, ground chiles, cumin, and salt and pepper to taste. Using your hands, mix well to blend. Form the mixture into 4 flattened patties of equal size.

Place the patties on the preheated grill (or stovetop pan) and grill for 5 minutes. Turn and grill for another 5 minutes for medium-well (160°F on an instant-read thermometer), or until cooked to the desired degree of doneness. Serve, topped with salsa.

*Nutritional Analysis per Serving: calories 225, carbohydrates 8 g, fiber 2 g, protein 22 g, fat 12 g, sodium 301 mg, sugar 4 g*

# *Tomato-Onion Salsa*

---

8 ounces Roma tomatoes, peeled, seeded, and coarsely chopped

1 small red onion, coarsely chopped

1 garlic clove, minced

½ teaspoon minced seeded hot red chile pepper, or to taste

½ teaspoon freshly squeezed lime juice

¼ cup chopped fresh cilantro

Salt and pepper

---

Combine the tomatoes and onion in a mixing bowl. Stir in the garlic and chile. When well combined, add the lime juice. Fold in the cilantro and season with salt and pepper to taste. If not serving immediately, cover and refrigerate for no more than 8 hours.

*Nutritional Analysis per Serving (¼ cup): calories 22, carbohydrates 5 g, fiber 1 g, protein 1 g, fat 0 g, sodium 77 mg, sugar 3 g*

# Grilled Veal Chops with Arugula

SERVES 4

This is a dish that you will want to make every month of the year. If you don't have a stovetop grill pan, please get one. Of course, they don't impart the scent of burning wood or charcoal to the meat, but they mark the meat beautifully and make it possible to grill all year round. This recipe works well with pork chops, too.

---

2 tablespoons extra-virgin olive oil

1 tablespoon freshly squeezed lemon juice

4 (7-ounce) veal chops

Salt and pepper

8 cups arugula

⅓ cup Balsamic Vinaigrette (page 36)

---

Preheat and oil the grill; alternatively, preheat a stovetop grill pan over medium-high heat.

Combine the olive oil and lemon juice and generously coat the chops with it. Season with salt and pepper to taste.

Place the chops on the preheated grill (or stovetop grill pan) and grill, turning occasionally, until an instant-read thermometer registers 130°F for medium, about 10 minutes, or until the desired doneness is reached. Remove from the grill and let rest for 5 minutes.

Place the arugula in a mixing bowl and drizzle about half of the vinaigrette over the leaves, tossing to coat.

Place an equal portion of the dressed arugula in the center of each of four dinner plates. Place a chop on top, drizzle with the remaining vinaigrette, and serve.

*Nutritional Analysis per Serving: calories 354, carbohydrates 2 g, fiber 0 g, protein 25 g, fat 28 g, sodium 455 mg, sugar 1 g*

# Veal Saltimbocca

This classic Mediterranean dish is popular in Italy, Spain, and parts of Greece. In Rome, the sauce is usually made with Marsala wine, which has some sweetness. You can also add capers to the finishing sauce for a hint of saltiness.

---

2 tablespoons plus 1 teaspoon chopped fresh sage

2 tablespoons chopped fresh rosemary

2 teaspoons minced garlic

4 (4-ounce) veal scallops

4 thin slices prosciutto

½ cup plus 3 tablespoons unsalted butter

2 tablespoons extra-virgin olive oil

Salt and pepper

½ cup dry white wine

2 tablespoons freshly squeezed lemon juice

---

Combine 2 tablespoons of the sage with the rosemary and garlic in a small mixing bowl.

Place the veal scallops on a clean, flat work surface. Working with one piece at a time, evenly cover each piece with the herb mixture. Then, cover the herb layer with a slice of prosciutto.

Starting at one end, firmly roll each veal scallop into a cigar shape. Using kitchen twine, tie each veal packet together by tying one loop of string around the center and another loop around the length of the packet.

Place ½ cup of the butter and the olive oil in a large frying pan over medium heat. When melted, season the veal packets with salt and pepper to taste and place them in the hot pan. Cook, turning occasionally, until nicely colored on all sides, about 5 minutes. Add the wine and lemon juice and bring to a simmer. Lower the heat, cover, and cook at a bare simmer until cooked through, about 20 minutes.

Using tongs, transfer the veal packets to a serving platter. Use kitchen scissors to carefully cut the ties.

Raise the heat to high under the frying pan and whisk in the remaining 3 tablespoons butter and 1 teaspoon sage. Taste and, if necessary, season with salt and pepper to taste. Pour over the veal and serve immediately.

*Nutritional Analysis per Serving: calories 644, carbohydrates 3 g, fiber 0 g, protein 32 g, fat 53 g, sodium 625 mg, sugar 0 g*

# Calf's Liver and Onions

SERVES 4

Liver is one of those meats that people either love or hate. No one likes it when it's overcooked, tough, and dry, but if you cook it carefully and quickly, liver is tender and mildly flavored. With the accent of sweet red onions it becomes a "can I have seconds" kind of dish.

---

6 tablespoons unsalted butter

3 tablespoons extra-virgin olive oil, plus more for brushing the pan

5 large red onions, cut crosswise into thin slices

Salt and pepper

3 tablespoons balsamic vinegar

1 pound calf's liver, cut into thick slices

---

Combine 4 tablespoons of the butter with 1 tablespoon of the olive oil in a large frying pan over medium heat. When melted, add the onions and season with salt and pepper to taste. Lower the heat and cook, stirring occasionally, until the onions have exuded most of their liquid, about 20 minutes. Add the vinegar and continue to cook for an additional 10 minutes. Stir in the remaining 2 tablespoons butter and, when melted, remove the pan from the heat, but cover it to keep warm.

Generously coat each slice of liver with the remaining 2 tablespoons olive oil. Season with salt and pepper to taste.

Preheat a stovetop grill pan over medium-high heat. When hot, brush with additional olive oil. Add the seasoned liver and cook, turning once, until nicely browned on each side, about 4 minutes. Do not overcook, as the liver will quickly toughen.

Remove from the heat and place the liver on a serving platter. Top with the warm onions and serve.

*Nutritional Analysis per Serving: calories 459, carbohydrates 22 g, fiber 3 g, protein 23 g, fat 32 g, sodium 648 mg, sugar 9 g*

# Roasted Leg of Lamb with Ginger Sauce

SERVES 6

Generally a leg of lamb is butterflied for grilling, and if you cook a small one, the whole leg can be grilled. I prefer roasting in a very hot oven for the first 15 minutes and then turning down the temperature to finish cooking. This recipe can be used for larger legs of lamb; roasting requires about 22 minutes per pound for rare or until a meat thermometer registers the degree of doneness you desire.

If you don't want to make the ginger sauce, mix some chopped fresh herbs (any combination you like) with the olive oil and rub into the meat instead. The herbs alone will add a hint of freshness to the juicy, deeply flavored lamb.

---

1 (3½-pound) leg of lamb, trimmed of excess fat

¼ cup extra-virgin olive oil

Salt and pepper

1 cup coarsely chopped peeled and seeded tomatoes

1 tablespoon grated ginger root

1 teaspoon chopped garlic

¼ cup dry white wine

2 tablespoons unsalted butter, at room temperature

¼ cup chopped fresh mint

---

Preheat the oven to 450°F.

Generously coat the lamb with the oil and season with salt and pepper to taste. Place on a rack in a small roasting pan and roast, turning occasionally, until nicely browned on all sides, about 15 minutes. Reduce the oven temperature to 325°F and continue to roast, without turning, until a meat thermometer registers 140° for rare, about 50 minutes, or until cooked to the desired degree of doneness (165°F will give you very well-done meat).

While the meat is roasting, prepare the sauce. Combine the tomatoes, ginger, and garlic in the bowl of a food processor fitted with the metal blade. Process, using quick on and off turns, to make a chunky mixture. Transfer to a small nonreactive saucepan over medium heat and bring to a simmer. Simmer, stirring frequently, for 5 minutes.

Add the wine and butter and season with salt and pepper to taste. Return to a simmer and simmer just long enough to allow the alcohol to evaporate slightly, about 5 minutes. Remove from the heat and fold in the mint. Cover to keep warm until ready to serve.

Remove the lamb from the oven and set aside to rest for a couple of minutes. Slice the meat across the grain and place on a platter. Serve with the warm sauce on the side.

*Nutritional Analysis per Serving: calories 371, carbohydrates 2 g, fiber 0 g, protein 36 g, fat 23 g, sodium 282 mg, sugar 1 g*

# Grilled Butterflied Leg of Lamb with Eggplant Compote

SERVES 6

Lamb and eggplant are two well-known partners in Greek cooking, and this recipe is an undemanding one that seals the marriage. Grilling makes it a warm-weather dish, but the lamb can also be roasted (see page 187) so quickly and effortlessly that it begs to be made year-round. Both the meat and the compote can be served at room temperature.

---

¾ cup extra-virgin olive oil

1 tablespoon freshly squeezed lemon juice

1 tablespoon celery seeds

1 teaspoon ground cumin

1 teaspoon smoked paprika

1 (3-pound) butterflied leg of lamb (see Note)

1 medium eggplant, cut crosswise into ½-inch-thick slices

2 large tomatoes, halved crosswise

Salt and pepper

½ cup finely chopped onion

¼ cup coarsely chopped green Greek olives

1 tablespoon roasted garlic puree (see page 64)

1 tablespoon red wine vinegar

2 teaspoons chopped capers

1 tablespoon chopped fresh flat-leaf parsley

---

Combine ½ cup of the olive oil with the lemon juice, celery seeds, cumin, and paprika in a small bowl. Generously coat the lamb with the oil mixture, reserving any remaining for later use. Set the lamb aside to marinate for 30 minutes.

Preheat and oil the grill; alternatively, preheat the oven to 400°F.

Generously coat the eggplant and tomatoes with the remaining ¼ cup olive oil. Season with salt and pepper to taste.

Place the vegetables on the preheated grill and grill the eggplant, turning occasionally, until nicely charred and just cooked through, about 8 minutes. Grill the tomatoes, skin-side down, without turning, just until slightly soft, about 4 minutes. Remove the vegetables from the grill and set aside. Do not turn off the grill.

Alternatively, place the eggplant and tomatoes on a rimmed baking sheet in the preheated oven and roast, turning occasionally, for 15 minutes for the eggplant and 10 minutes for the tomatoes. Do not turn off the oven if you are using it to roast the lamb.

Season the lamb with salt and pepper to taste and place on the hot grill. Grill, turning occasionally and brushing with the reserved oil mixture, for 12 minutes. Move the lamb to the cooler part of the grill. Cover and continue to grill, turning and brushing with the oil mixture from time to time, until an instant-read thermometer inserted into the thickest part reads 140°F for rare, about 18 minutes, or until cooked to the desired degree of doneness. Alternatively, place the lamb on a rack in a roasting pan in the preheated oven and roast until it reaches the same degree of doneness as for grilling, about 30 minutes.

While the meat is cooking, make the compote. Place the eggplant and tomatoes in the bowl of a food processor fitted with the metal blade. Process, using quick on and off turns, until just barely chopped.

Transfer to a mixing bowl and stir in the onion, olives, garlic, vinegar, and capers. Season with salt and pepper to taste and set aside for 30 minutes to allow the flavors to blend. Fold in the parsley and transfer to a serving bowl.

Remove the lamb from the grill or the oven and set aside to rest for a couple of minutes. Slice the meat across the grain and place on a platter. Serve with the compote on the side.

**NOTE:** A butterflied leg of lamb is simply a leg of lamb from which the bone has been removed and then the meat split down but not through the center to open it up. The meat is then flattened slightly to resemble a butterfly. Most butchers will be happy to do this for you.

*Nutritional Analysis per Serving: calories 450, carbohydrates 10 g, fiber 3 g, protein 43 g, fat 27 g, sodium 469 mg, sugar 4 g*

# Lamb and Fennel with Mint Salad

SERVES 4

Here is another lamb recipe that is scented with the flavors of Greece—fennel, feta, olive oil, mint, and oregano (if you can find it, Greek oregano has wonderful qualities of its own). This is a light and beautiful dish that works well as both a weekday dinner and a "company's coming" sensation.

---

3 large fennel bulbs

¼ cup extra-virgin olive oil

2 tablespoons red wine vinegar

2 tablespoons chopped fresh oregano

Salt and cracked black pepper

1 (1¼-pound) boneless lamb loin

1½ cups fresh mint leaves

5 ounces feta cheese, crumbled

1 tablespoon freshly grated orange zest

1 tablespoon freshly squeezed lemon juice

2 tablespoons toasted pumpkin seeds

---

Preheat the oven to 400°F. Line a baking sheet with parchment paper and set aside.

Trim off any dark or damaged pieces from the fennel bulbs, leaving the bulb intact and reserving the fronds. Using a sharp knife, cut the fennel bulbs lengthwise into 8 slices total. Chop enough of the fronds to yield 1 tablespoon, reserving the remainder in their feathery state for the salad (you will need about ⅓ cup).

Combine the oil, vinegar, and oregano with the chopped fennel fronds. Season the mixture with salt and cracked pepper to taste. Generously coat the fennel slices and the lamb with the seasoned oil.

Lay out the fennel slices on the prepared baking sheet and place the lamb on a rack in a small roasting pan. Transfer both to the preheated oven and roast until the fennel is nicely colored and cooked through and the lamb is cooked to 140°F for rare, about 12 minutes, or until cooked to the desired degree of doneness.

While the fennel and lamb are cooking, make the salad. Combine the mint with ⅓ cup of the reserved fennel fronds and the feta in a serving bowl. Sprinkle the orange zest and lemon juice over the top and season with salt and pepper to taste. Toss to coat.

Remove the lamb from the oven and set aside to rest for 5 minutes. Cut the lamb crosswise into thick slices.

Place two slices of the roasted fennel in the center of each of four dinner plates. Top with an equal portion of the sliced lamb. Mound the salad on top, sprinkle with pumpkin seeds, and serve immediately.

*Nutritional Analysis per Serving: calories 565, carbohydrates 11 g, fiber 4 g, protein 34 g, fat 44 g, sodium 720 mg, sugar 5 g*

# Braised Lamb Shanks with Green Olives

SERVES 4

In recent years, braised lamb shanks have become the go-to comfort food. They are meaty, flavorful, and easy to cook. You can put them together in the morning and go about your day while they simmer away. Then, dinner is on the table in minutes.

---

3 tablespoons extra-virgin olive oil

4 whole lamb shanks

Salt and pepper

1 cup chopped leek (including some of the green part)

1 tablespoon minced garlic

1 celery rib, peeled and chopped

1 cup diced rutabaga

1 cup dry red wine

3 cups chicken stock (page 33) or low-sodium chicken broth

1 (28-ounce) can diced tomatoes, with their juice

1 teaspoon minced fresh rosemary

1 teaspoon minced fresh thyme

1 teaspoon minced fresh basil

1 teaspoon minced fresh flat-leaf parsley

1½ cups pitted green olives

---

Preheat the oven to 350°F.

Heat the oil in a Dutch oven over medium heat. Season the lamb shanks with salt and pepper to taste and add them to the hot oil. Sear, turning occasionally, until all sides are browned, about 10 minutes. Using tongs, transfer the browned shanks to a platter.

Remove all but 1 tablespoon of fat from the pan. Add the leek and garlic and sauté for 3 minutes. Stir in the celery and rutabaga and continue cooking for another 4 minutes.

Add the red wine to the pan, raise the heat, and bring to a boil. Boil, stirring constantly with a wooden spoon to release all of the browned bits in the bottom of the pan, until the wine begins to evaporate, about 7 minutes.

Add the chicken stock and again bring to a boil. Stir in the tomatoes, rosemary, thyme, basil, and parsley and once again bring to a boil.

Return the shanks to the pan and season with salt and pepper to taste. Cover, transfer to the preheated oven, and braise for 1 hour. Uncover, add the olives, and continue to braise until the meat is almost falling off the bone, about 1 hour more. Remove from the oven and serve.

*Nutritional Analysis per Serving: calories 472, carbohydrates 20 g, fiber 3 g, protein 30 g, fat 25 g, sodium 768 mg, sugar 9 g*

# Quick "Moussaka"

SERVES 4

Moussaka, a traditional Greek dish, is made with a rich béchamel sauce along with lamb, tomatoes, eggplant, breadcrumbs, and lots of sweet spice. This is a very modest version that takes no time to put together and is just as delicious reheated the next day. If you love cinnamon and allspice, you can add about ½ teaspoon of each to the lamb mixture for a slightly different flavor. Either way, this "moussaka" goes well with a tossed green salad on the side.

---

2 tablespoons avocado oil

1 large zucchini

1 pound ground lamb

1 tablespoon chopped fresh flat-leaf parsley

1 teaspoon chopped fresh oregano, plus more for optional garnish

1 teaspoon minced garlic

1 large egg

Salt and pepper

5 ounces crumbled feta cheese

8 eggplant slices (about 6 inches long and ⅓ inch thick)

1 cup sheep's milk ricotta cheese

1 cup shredded mozzarella cheese

---

Preheat the oven to 350°F. Line a large baking pan with parchment paper. Generously coat the paper with 1 tablespoon of the avocado oil and set aside.

Grate the zucchini and place it in a clean kitchen towel. Tightly twist the towel together and squeeze out as much of the liquid as you can.

Combine the drained zucchini with the lamb, parsley, oregano, and garlic, stirring to blend. Add the egg, season with salt and pepper to taste, and use your hands to blend the mixture well. Add the feta and carefully mix — you want to blend but not completely mash the cheese.

Lay out 4 eggplant slices in a single layer in the prepared baking pan. Top each piece with an equal portion of the lamb, patting down to make a smooth, even coating. Place another slice of eggplant on top. Using a pastry brush, generously coat the eggplant with the remaining 1 tablespoon avocado oil.

Combine the ricotta and mozzarella in a medium bowl. When mixed, place an equal portion on top of the oiled eggplant slices, again smoothing to make an even cover.

Transfer to the preheated oven and bake until the top is golden brown and the lamb is completely cooked, about 45 minutes. Remove from the oven and sprinkle with additional oregano, if desired. Place an individual "moussaka" on each of four dinner plates and serve.

*Nutritional Analysis per Serving: calories 657, carbohydrates 22 g, fiber 2 g, protein 48 g, fat 52 g, sodium 780 mg, sugar 6 g*

# Stuffed Pork Loin

SERVES 6

Free-range pork has a much richer flavor and deeper texture than commercially raised pork. The walnuts and walnut oil add a unique taste that marries well with the pork. This recipe is a wonderful Sunday supper or dinner party dish that can be served with more sautéed Swiss chard on the side.

---

1 (3-pound) boneless pork loin

3 tablespoons unsalted butter

3 cups chopped Swiss chard

½ cup minced onion

1 teaspoon minced garlic

Salt and pepper

2 tablespoons walnut oil

1 cup dry white wine

½ cup chopped raw walnuts

---

Preheat the oven to 400°F.

Using a sharp knife, carefully cut the pork loin open to make a neat, flat solid piece of meat. This is best done by cutting from one side into the center (without cutting through to the edge) and then carefully folding the cut flap out. Then, cut from the interior out through the thicker piece to open another flap. Gently push down to flatten the entire piece out. Cover with plastic wrap and let the pork come to room temperature.

Melt the butter in a medium frying pan over medium heat. Add the chard, onion, and garlic and sauté until softened, about 4 minutes. Season with salt and pepper to taste.

Uncover the pork and carefully cover with an even layer of the chard stuffing, leaving about an inch around the edges. Roll up from the bottom to make a neat log. Using butcher's twine, tie the roll closed. Rub the exterior with the walnut oil and again season with salt and pepper to taste.

Transfer the loin to a roasting pan and pour in the wine. Place in the preheated oven and roast until nicely colored, about 30 minutes. Add the walnuts, lower the heat to 375°F, and roast until an instant-read thermometer reads 160°F when inserted into the thickest part of the loin, about 1 hour more. Remove from the oven and let rest for 15 minutes.

Untie and cut the loin crosswise into thin slices. Drizzle the pan juices over the sliced meat, sprinkle with the walnuts, and serve.

*Nutritional Analysis per Serving: calories 407, carbohydrates 4 g, fiber 2 g, protein 46 g, fat 23 g, sodium 356 mg, sugar 1 g*

# Pork Tenderloin with Sweet Spiced Onion Jam

This is a simple dish that is simply delish! Pork tenderloin cooks in no time and the jam can be made in advance, so this makes for a quick weeknight dinner. Be careful when you roast the tenderloin; it will be tough if overcooked.

1 (1¼-pound) pork tenderloin

1 tablespoon extra-virgin olive oil

Salt and pepper

½ cup Sweet Spiced Onion Jam (recipe follows)

Preheat the oven to 400°F.

Using your hands, rub the entire tenderloin with the olive oil. Generously season with salt and pepper.

Place the tenderloin in a large, oven-safe frying pan over high heat. Sear, turning frequently, until all sides are browned, about 5 minutes. Transfer to the preheated oven and roast until an instant-read thermometer inserted in the center reads 145°F, about 20 minutes. Remove from the oven and let rest for 5 minutes before cutting crosswise into thin slices.

Spread the onion jam on a serving platter and then place the pork in slightly overlapping slices down the center. Serve immediately.

*Nutritional Analysis per Serving (includes 2 tablespoons onion jam): calories 221, carbohydrates 4 g, fiber 1 g, protein 27 g, fat 10 g, sodium 241 mg, sugar 2 g*

# *Sweet Spiced Onion Jam*

MAKES ABOUT 3 CUPS

---

½ cup unsalted butter

10 cups sliced red onions

3 tablespoons balsamic vinegar

2 teaspoons ground cinnamon

½ teaspoon ground cloves

½ teaspoon ground cardamom

Salt and pepper

---

Melt the butter in a large sauté pan over medium-low heat. Add the onions, lower the heat, cover, and cook, stirring occasionally, until very soft, about 30 minutes. Stir in the vinegar, cinnamon, cloves, and cardamom, season with salt and pepper to taste, and continue to cook until the onions are jam-like and almost falling apart, about 15 minutes more.

Remove from the heat and serve, or allow to cool and store, covered, in the refrigerator for up to 1 week.

*Nutritional Analysis per Serving (2 tablespoons): calories 41, carbohydrates 4 g, fiber 1 g, protein 1 g, fat 3 g, sodium 38 mg, sugar 2 g*

# Grilled Pork Chops with Salsa Verde

SERVES 4

What could be easier than throwing a few chops on the grill? Nothing that I know of, but I do like to take a little extra time to brine the meat in a salty-herby mix. This tenderizes the meat and adds some flavor. The salsa keeps well for a few days, covered and refrigerated, and can be used with almost any type of meat or fish.

3 tablespoons salt, plus more for seasoning

4 flat-leaf parsley sprigs

4 thyme sprigs

4 (5-ounce) thick-cut pork chops

Pepper

½ cup Salsa Verde (recipe follows)

Combine the salt, parsley, and thyme in a resealable plastic bag. Add the chops and pour in enough cold water to completely cover them. Seal the bag and refrigerate for 1 hour.

When ready to cook, preheat and oil the grill. Alternatively, preheat a stovetop grill pan over medium-high heat.

Drain the chops and pat them dry. Season with salt and pepper to taste and place on the preheated grill (or stovetop grill pan). Grill, turning occasionally to nicely mark the meat, until an instant-read thermometer reads 145°F, about 15 minutes. Remove from the grill and let rest for 10 minutes. Serve with salsa verde on the side.

*Nutritional Analysis per Serving (includes 2 tablespoons salsa verde): calories 199, carbohydrates 1 g, fiber 0 g, protein 20 g, fat 13 g, sodium 704 mg, sugar 0 g*

# Salsa Verde

---

½ bunch curly spinach, finely chopped (stems included)

1 shallot, finely chopped

2 teaspoons finely chopped scallion

1 teaspoon freshly grated orange zest

½ cup extra-virgin olive oil

1 tablespoon red wine vinegar

Salt and pepper

---

Combine the spinach, shallot, scallion, and orange zest in a mixing bowl. Add the olive oil and vinegar and season with salt and pepper to taste. Taste and, if a zestier flavor is desired, add more vinegar. (If you decide to do all of this in a food processor, do not overprocess; you want some texture and you don't want to emulsify the oil.)

*Nutritional Analysis per Serving (2 tablespoons): calories 64, carbohydrates 1 g, fiber 0 g, protein 0 g, fat 7 g, sodium 81 mg, sugar 0 g*

# Gruyère-Glazed Pork Chops

SERVES 4

Only the French would have thought to glaze meat with cheese! The chops must be fully cooked before being glazed, and the glaze should be golden brown and bubbly as the chops come to the table.

1 large egg yolk

1 cup grated Gruyère cheese (about 4 ounces)

1 tablespoon Dijon mustard

1 tablespoon almond milk

1 tablespoon chopped fresh chives

4 (5-ounce) pork loin chops

Salt and pepper

1 tablespoon coconut oil

Combine the egg yolk, cheese, mustard, milk, and chives in a small mixing bowl. Using a wooden spoon, stir and mash until completely soft and blended. Set aside.

Season the chops with salt and pepper to taste.

Heat the oil in a large frying pan over medium-high heat. Add the seasoned chops and fry, turning occasionally, until both sides are nicely browned, about 15 minutes.

Preheat the broiler.

Remove the chops from the frying pan and carefully coat one side of each chop with an equal portion of the cheese mixture.

Place the coated chops on a broiler pan under the preheated broiler. Broil until the cheese is golden brown, bubbling, and glazed, about 3 minutes. Remove from the broiler and serve.

*Nutritional Analysis per Serving: calories 328, carbohydrates 2 g, fiber 0 g, protein 35 g, fat 20 g, sodium 243 mg, sugar 0 g*

# Adobo Pork

SERVES 4

This recipe is based on a traditional pork dish from the Philippines, where both pork and coconut make frequent appearances on the dinner table. The heat of the big dose of pepper is tempered by the coconut milk. I like to serve this dish with Fried Green Plantains (page 150).

---

1½ tablespoons coconut oil

1 medium onion, sliced

1 tablespoon minced garlic

1 (1-pound) pork tenderloin, cut into bite-size pieces

1 tablespoon pepper

¾ cup water

1 tablespoon white vinegar

2 bay leaves

1½ cups unsweetened coconut milk

2 tablespoons toasted unsweetened coconut flakes

---

Heat the oil in a large saucepan over medium heat. Add the onion and garlic and cook, stirring frequently, until beginning to color, about 5 minutes Do not allow the garlic to burn. Add the pork, season with the pepper, and cook just until the pork begins to color, about 5 minutes more.

Stir in the water, vinegar, and bay leaves. Bring to a simmer and simmer until the pork is just cooked, about 20 minutes. Add the coconut milk and continue to cook until the pork is very tender, about 10 minutes more. Remove from the heat and serve, sprinkled with the toasted coconut.

*Nutritional Analysis per Serving: calories 356, carbohydrates 8 g, fiber 1 g, protein 23 g, fat 26 g, sodium 72 mg, sugar 1 g*

# Stir-Fried Pork with Watercress

SERVES 4

We often think of watercress as that sprig of garnish on a restaurant plate, but it is far more useful than that. It can be sautéed for a side vegetable to go with almost any meat, but you must take care not to overcook it. In this recipe, the hot meat wilts it just enough, leaving a little crunch and lots of spice.

---

2 tablespoons coconut oil

1 tablespoon minced garlic

1 tablespoon minced ginger root

1 pound pork tenderloin, cut into bite-size pieces

Salt and pepper

1 pound watercress, tough stems removed

½ cup sunflower seeds

1 teaspoon freshly grated orange zest

---

Heat the oil in a wok or large frying pan over medium-high heat. Add the garlic and ginger and cook, stirring constantly, until lightly colored, about 2 minutes. Add the pork and season with salt and pepper to taste. Cook, occasionally tossing and turning, until the pork is no longer pink and has begun to color around the edges, about 5 minutes. Remove from the heat and toss in the watercress, sunflower seeds, and orange zest. Serve immediately.

*Nutritional Analysis per Serving: calories 300, carbohydrates 6 g, fiber 2 g, protein 28 g, fat 19 g, sodium 385 mg, sugar 1 g*

# Slow-Roasted Spareribs

SERVES 4

Who thinks of spareribs in the middle of winter? With this recipe you will, although you can also slow-roast these on the grill in the summer. You can easily vary the spices for the rub using any that appeal to you, but always add a little heat by including ground chiles or cayenne. The heat sinks into the ribs and turns them into a tantalizing lick-your-fingers dish.

---

4 pounds spareribs

1 tablespoon ground dried chiles, such as ancho

1½ teaspoons ground cumin

1½ teaspoons black pepper

1 teaspoon salt

1 teaspoon ground cinnamon

1 teaspoon cayenne pepper, or to taste

---

Place the spareribs on a rimmed baking sheet.

Combine the ground chiles, cumin, black pepper, salt, cinnamon, and cayenne in a small mixing bowl until well blended. Using your hands, coat both sides of the ribs with the spice rub. Cover with plastic wrap and marinate at room temperature for 1 hour or in the refrigerator for up to 8 hours. If refrigerated, bring to room temperature before roasting.

Preheat the oven to 300°F.

Unwrap the ribs and cover with aluminum foil, taking care to seal it all around. Place in the preheated oven and roast until the ribs are completely cooked through and almost falling off the bone, about 2½ hours. Remove from the oven and serve, with plenty of napkins.

*Nutritional Analysis per Serving: calories 711, carbohydrates 2 g, fiber 1 g, protein 52 g, fat 54 g, sodium 746 mg, sugar 0 g*

# Poultry

---

# Perfect Roast Chicken

SERVES 4

You have to think a bit ahead to make this chicken, but it is well worth the time. You will get moist, juicy meat and unbelievably crisp skin. I like to put a couple of lemon halves in the pan for the last 15 minutes and then squirt some hot lemon juice on the meat when I serve it.

---

1 (3½-pound) chicken
Salt

---

Rinse the chicken under cold running water and pat it dry. Generously coat the exterior with salt—all of the skin should be covered.

Place the salted chicken in a shallow bowl, cover with plastic wrap, and place in the refrigerator for 48 hours.

About 1 hour before you're ready to roast, preheat the oven to 450°F. Remove the chicken from the refrigerator and set it aside to come to room temperature.

About 30 minutes before roasting, place a small roasting pan in the oven to heat it up.

Uncover the chicken, push off any remaining salt, and carefully pat the skin dry.

Place a rack in the roasting pan and then place the salted chicken on the rack, breast-side up. Roast until the chicken is cooked through and the skin is golden brown and very crisp, about 45 minutes. Remove from the oven and let rest for 10 minutes before carving. Serve.

*Nutritional Analysis per Serving: calories 451, carbohydrates 0 g, fiber 0 g, protein 52 g, fat 26 g, sodium 735 mg, sugar 0 g*

# Pesto-Roasted Chicken

This is an extraordinarily flavorful roast chicken. It takes a little patience to stuff the seasoned ricotta under the skin, but the result is well worth the effort. The extra pesto you'll make keeps well and is terrific on roasted vegetables or as a seasoning for a basic vinaigrette.

---

1 (3½-pound) chicken

2 cups fresh sheep's milk ricotta

⅓ cup Pesto (recipe follows)

Salt and pepper

⅔ cup unsalted butter, melted

1 lemon

---

Preheat the oven to 400°F.

Rinse the chicken under cold running water and pat dry. Place it on a clean cutting board.

Combine the ricotta with the pesto, beating to blend completely. Taste and, if necessary, season with salt and pepper to taste.

Using your fingertips, carefully push back the skin from both sides of the chicken breast to loosen it from the flesh. Working downward, push your fingertips into the leg to loosen the skin around the thigh and leg on both sides. Then, working with just a small handful of the ricotta mixture at a time, scoop it up and begin patting it over the flesh wherever you have loosened the skin. You should end up with a smooth, even layer of ricotta under the skin.

Place the melted butter in a small bowl. Using a zester, remove the zest from the lemon and add it to the butter. Cut the lemon in half crosswise and place it in the cavity of the chicken.

Pull the chicken legs up and against the body and tie the ends of the legs together with kitchen twine. Lift the wing tips up and tuck them under the chicken. Using a pastry brush, lightly coat the exterior of the chicken with the lemon-scented butter and season with salt and pepper to taste.

Place the chicken, breast-side up, on a rack in a small roasting pan and transfer to the preheated oven. Roast, basting frequently with the lemon-scented butter, until the skin is golden brown, the ricotta has puffed somewhat, and a meat thermometer inserted into the thickest part of the thigh reads 160°F, about 45 minutes. Remove the chicken from the oven and let rest for 10 minutes before carving. Serve.

*Nutritional Analysis per Serving: calories 622, carbohydrates 7 g, fiber 0 g, protein 59 g, fat 43 g, sodium 511 mg, sugar 1 g*

# Pesto

---

2 tightly packed cups fresh basil leaves

¼ cup toasted pine nuts

1 teaspoon chopped garlic

1 cup extra-virgin olive oil

½ cup grated Parmesan cheese

Salt and pepper

---

Combine the basil, pine nuts, and garlic in the bowl of a food processor fitted with the metal blade and process just until chopped. With the motor running, begin slowly adding about half of the olive oil through the feed tube, processing until blended. Don't overprocess, as you want to see tiny bits of basil. Scrape the puree from the processor bowl into a small mixing bowl. Stir in the cheese and season with salt and pepper to taste. Beat in the remaining olive oil until a thick puree forms.

If not using immediately, scrape the pesto into a clean, glass container. Smooth the top and then cover it with a thin layer of olive oil; this will keep the pesto from discoloring. Store in the refrigerator until ready to use, up to 2 weeks, or in the freezer for up to 3 months (thaw before using).

*Nutritional Analysis per Serving: calories 123, carbohydrates 0 g, fiber 0 g, protein 2 g, fat 13 g, sodium 63 mg, sugar 0 g*

# Grilled Coconut-Sesame Chicken with Jicama-Cucumber Relish

SERVES 4

Chicken thighs work well on the grill because they have more fat than the ubiquitous chicken breasts and, when cooked, are juicier and far more flavorful. If you don't have an outdoor grill, this recipe can be made year-round using a stovetop grill pan. The marinade also works with pork, shrimp, or turkey, and the relish is great with almost anything you can imagine, from roasts to barbecue.

---

1 cup unsweetened coconut milk

2 tablespoons toasted sesame oil

2 tablespoons minced scallion

1 tablespoon chopped fresh mint

1 tablespoon sesame seeds

1 tablespoon freshly squeezed lime juice

8 small bone-in, skin-on chicken thighs (about 1½ pounds total)

Salt and pepper

½ cup Jicama-Cucumber Relish (recipe follows)

---

Combine the coconut milk, sesame oil, scallion, mint, sesame seeds, and lime juice in a large resealable plastic bag. Add the chicken, seal, and roll around to evenly coat. Refrigerate for at least 1 hour or up to 12 hours.

Preheat and oil the grill; alternatively, heat a nonstick stovetop grill pan over medium-high heat.

Remove the chicken from the bag and season with salt and pepper to taste. Place on the hot grill (or stovetop grill pan) and grill, turning frequently, until just cooked through, about 12 minutes. Do not overcook or the meat will be dry and tough.

Remove from the grill and transfer to a serving platter. Serve with the relish on the side.

*Nutritional Analysis per Serving: calories 412, carbohydrates 4 g, fiber 1 g, protein 24 g, fat 34 g, sodium 296 mg, sugar 0 g*

## *Jicama-Cucumber Relish*

MAKES ABOUT 2¼ CUPS

---

1 cup finely chopped jicama

1 cup finely chopped seedless cucumber

¼ cup chopped fresh mint

2 tablespoons chopped scallion

1 teaspoon freshly grated orange zest

3 tablespoons white vinegar

½ teaspoon stevia powder

Salt

---

Combine the jicama, cucumber, mint, scallion, and orange zest in a small mixing bowl. Add the vinegar and stevia. Season with salt to taste and stir to combine. Cover and refrigerate for at least 30 minutes to allow the flavors to blend, or up to 3 days.

*Nutritional Analysis per Serving (2 tablespoons): calories 3, carbohydrates 1 g, fiber 0 g, protein 0 g, fat 0 g, sodium 49 mg, sugar 0 g*

Grilled Parmesan Tomatoes (page 148)

London Broil with Grilled Mushrooms (page 170)

Grilled Pork Chops with Salsa Verde (page 202)

Grilled Coconut-Sesame Chicken with Jicama-Cucumber Relish (page 215)

Garlic Shrimp (page 254)

Salmon Roasted in Butter and Almonds (page 237)

Cauliflower "Hummus" (page 294)

Vegetable Chips (page 275)

Chocolate Almond Cake (page 307)

Raw Chia Seed Pudding
(page 316)

Coconut Burs
(page 301)

# Chicken with Forty Cloves of Garlic

SERVES 4

This is a classic dish from Provence. I wonder if the original cook labeled it with the forty cloves of garlic to scare off future cooks from this unique recipe. Interestingly, the garlic mellows as it cooks and becomes quite sweet; some cooks use up to one hundred cloves. The resulting sauce is buttery and mildly fragrant and takes everyday chicken to new heights.

3 tablespoons avocado oil, plus more for greasing pan

1 (3½-pound) chicken, cut into 8 pieces

Salt and pepper

40 garlic cloves, peeled

⅓ cup dry vermouth

1 teaspoon dried tarragon

¾ cup chicken stock (page 33) or low-sodium chicken broth

1 teaspoon freshly squeezed lemon juice

1 tablespoon chopped fresh chives, for garnish

Preheat the oven to 400°F. Lightly coat the interior of a small roasting pan with avocado oil. Set aside.

Heat the oil in a large, heavy-bottomed saucepan over medium heat. Season the chicken pieces with salt and pepper to taste and add them to the saucepan, skin-side down. Sear, turning occasionally, until nicely browned on all sides, about 12 minutes. Using tongs, transfer the chicken to the roasting pan. Leave the saucepan on the heat.

Place all of the garlic cloves in the saucepan and cook, stirring frequently, just until they begin to brown, about 5 minutes. Add the vermouth and tarragon and cook, scraping up the browned bits from the bottom of the pot, until reduced by half, about 4 minutes.

Add the stock, raise the heat, and bring to a boil. Boil just until the garlic has softened, about 5 minutes. Using a slotted spoon, transfer 10 of the garlic cloves to the roasting pan. Using a kitchen fork, mash the remaining garlic cloves into the liquid in the saucepan.

Pour the sauce over the chicken and transfer to the preheated oven. Roast until the chicken is cooked through and the sauce is thick and flavorful, about 20 minutes.

Remove from the oven and transfer the chicken to a serving platter. Add the lemon juice to the sauce in the roasting pan, stirring to blend. Taste and, if necessary, season with additional salt and pepper. Pour the sauce over the chicken and garnish with the chives. Serve immediately.

*Nutritional Analysis per Serving: calories 574, carbohydrates 9 g, fiber 1 g, protein 53 g, fat 33 g, sodium 588 mg, sugar 2 g*

# Chicken Breasts Stuffed with Swiss Chard and Goat Cheese

SERVES 4

Company coming? Put this wonderful recipe together early in the day and pop it in the oven while drinks are served. You'll have dinner on the table in minutes without spending much time in the kitchen at all.

If Swiss chard is not available, use spinach or kale, and the goat cheese can be replaced with any soft cheese you like.

---

1 tablespoon extra-virgin olive oil

1 shallot, minced

8 ounces Swiss chard, tough stems removed and leaves finely chopped

Salt and pepper

1 teaspoon freshly grated orange zest

4 (5-ounce) boneless, skin-on chicken breasts

4 ounces soft goat cheese

2 tablespoons unsalted butter, melted

---

Preheat the oven to 400°F.

Heat the oil in a large skillet over medium-low heat. Add the shallot and cook, stirring frequently, until soft, about 2 minutes. Add the chard and season with salt and pepper to taste. Cook, stirring occasionally, until the chard has wilted and any liquid has evaporated, about 5 minutes. Remove from the heat and stir in the orange zest. Set aside to cool.

Working with one breast at a time, use a small, sharp knife to cut a pocket into the chicken. Begin at the thickest part and cut into the center but not through the entire breast; continue the length of the breast until you have a deep pocket. Season the pockets with salt and pepper to taste.

When the chard has cooled, crumble the goat cheese and toss it into the chard. Using your fingers, fill each pocket with an equal portion of the chard-cheese mixture. Close the pockets by sticking a couple of toothpicks into the edge. Generously coat the exterior of each breast with melted butter and season with salt and pepper to taste.

Place the stuffed breasts in a small roasting pan. Transfer to the preheated oven and bake until the meat is cooked through and the skin golden brown, about 15 minutes. Remove from the oven and serve.

*Nutritional Analysis per Serving: calories 382, carbohydrates 6 g, fiber 1 g, protein 37 g, fat 24 g, sodium 596 mg, sugar 3 g*

# Jerk Chicken

This is as close to an outdoor vendor on a Jamaican beach as you can get in your own backyard (or kitchen). Blisteringly hot, spicy, and juicy is just what you'll get here. If you don't have a grill, the chicken may be cooked on a stovetop grill pan or in a preheated 375°F oven for about the same amount of time.

You can make as much of the seasoning as you like as it will keep, covered and refrigerated, for up to 1 month. Jamaicans prefer their seasoning to be made with lots and lots of fresh Scotch bonnet chiles, which are extremely hot. You can achieve the amount of heat you desire by adding or decreasing the amount of fresh chiles. Just remember that you are looking for the perfect balance of heat, spice, and acid.

½ cup freshly squeezed lime juice

2 tablespoons white vinegar

2 tablespoons minced seeded hot chile, such as Scotch bonnet, or to taste

1 tablespoon freshly grated orange zest

2 tablespoons mustard seeds

1 tablespoon ground thyme

1 tablespoon ground allspice

1 teaspoon ground cloves

½ teaspoon ground nutmeg

Salt and pepper

6 bone-in, skin-on chicken thighs

1 lime, cut into wedges, for serving, optional

Preheat and oil the grill.

Combine the lime juice and vinegar in the blender jar. Add the chile and orange zest and process to blend. Add the mustard seeds, thyme, allspice, cloves, and nutmeg and process to a thick, sauce-like consistency. If it's too thick, add additional citrus juice or vinegar.

Lightly coat each thigh with the spice mixture and season with salt and pepper to taste. Place the thighs, skin-side down, on the outer rim of the pre-heated grill (slightly away from direct heat), cover, and grill until they are crisp and almost cooked through, about 10 minutes. Turn and continue to grill until thoroughly cooked, about 8 minutes more. Remove from the grill and serve with wedges of lime, if desired.

**VARIATIONS:** This seasoning is excellent on any type of chicken or turkey, pork chops, pork tenderloin, whole fish, or fish fillets.

*Nutritional Analysis per Serving: calories 349, carbohydrates 3 g, fiber 1 g, protein 31 g, fat 23 g, sodium 312 mg, sugar 0 g*

# Baked Chicken Parcels

SERVES 4

This is a super dish for entertaining, as the little parcels can be put together in advance and baked just before serving. In that case, make the parcels from parchment paper, as it is a bit more attractive at the table than foil. This recipe can also be used with firm white fish, such as halibut.

---

4 (5-ounce) boneless, skinless chicken breast halves (see Note)

2 teaspoons chopped fresh basil

1 teaspoon chopped fresh thyme

8 oil-packed sun-dried tomatoes, well drained

2 tablespoons sliced black or green Greek olives

4 rosemary sprigs

2 tablespoons unsalted butter, divided into 4 pats

Salt and pepper

1 tablespoon chia seeds

---

Preheat the oven to 350°F.

Tear four pieces of aluminum foil large enough to completely enclose a chicken breast—they will need to be about a foot long. Alternatively, cut four pieces of parchment paper into a heart shape, each about 12 inches long.

If using foil, lay the four pieces out on the counter. Place a chicken breast in the center of each one. Season each breast with equal amounts of basil and thyme. Place 2 sun-dried tomatoes on top of each piece of chicken. Add a few slices of olive and a sprig of rosemary, place a pat of butter on top, and season with salt and pepper to taste. Finally sprinkle chia seeds over all. Fold the foil up and around the chicken and tightly crimp the edges to completely enclose the chicken.

If using parchment paper, place the breast on one side of the heart shape near the center and layer the ingredients on top, as above. Fold the other side of the paper up and over the chicken so the two sides meet. Starting at one end of the half heart, begin folding the edges in and over to make a tightly crimped seal as you work your way around to firmly enclose the chicken. If desired, you can wet the inner edge of the paper with a bit of egg white before folding it over the chicken to ensure a tight seal.

Place the parcels in a baking pan in the preheated oven and bake for 20 minutes. Place a packet on each of four dinner plates, to be opened at the table.

**NOTE:** Packaged supermarket chicken breasts are often huge, weighing in at 12 ounces or more. This is just another reason why you should purchase humanely raised, free-range, organic chicken; the breasts will usually weigh in at a more reasonable 5 to 6 ounces.

**VARIATIONS:** Rather than in packets, the recipe may be made in a slow cooker. You will need to add ¼ cup chicken broth or water and cook on low for about 3 hours. Any herb or spice can be used at your discretion, and the sun-dried tomatoes can easily be replaced with peeled and chopped fresh Roma tomatoes.

*Nutritional Analysis per Serving: calories 235, carbohydrates 4 g, fiber 2 g, protein 30 g, fat 11 g, sodium 527 mg, sugar 1 g*

# Chicken Curry with Cilantro Chutney

SERVES 4

This dish has all the flavors of Southeast Asian cooking without the work of making an authentic curry. If you choose to use it, the toasted flaked coconut will add a touch of sweetness and crunch to offset the heat. The chutney offers a cooling element, and the vivid green makes an inviting contrast to the vibrant orange curry. Steamed Cauliflower "Couscous" (page 159) would make a fabulous base for the curry as it would absorb much of the tasty sauce.

1 pound boneless, skinless chicken breasts and/or thighs, cut into bite-size pieces

Salt

Cayenne pepper

1 tablespoon clarified butter (see page 42), ghee, or unsalted butter

1 cup finely chopped onion

1 teaspoon minced garlic

2 teaspoons hot curry powder

½ teaspoon ground turmeric

1 cup chicken stock (page 33) or low-sodium chicken broth, plus more if needed

½ cup unsweetened coconut milk

½ cup sliced water chestnuts

1 cup thawed and well-drained frozen chopped spinach

3 tablespoons toasted coconut flakes, for optional garnish

¼ cup Cilantro Chutney (recipe follows), optional

Season the chicken with salt and cayenne pepper to taste.

Heat the clarified butter in a large, nonstick frying pan over medium heat. Add the chicken and cook, stirring frequently, just until it begins to color, about 4 minutes. Using a slotted spoon, remove the chicken from the pan and set aside.

Add the onion, garlic, curry powder, and turmeric to the pan, stirring to combine. Cook, stirring constantly, just until the onion has wilted, about 3 minutes.

Return the chicken to the pan and add the stock and coconut milk. Taste and, if necessary, add additional salt and cayenne. Stir in the water chestnuts and spinach, cover, and cook until the chicken has cooked through and the sauce has thickened, about 12 minutes.

Remove from the heat and serve, sprinkled with the toasted coconut flakes and the chutney passed on the side, if desired.

*Nutritional Analysis per Serving (includes 1 tablespoon chutney): calories 279, carbohydrates 11 g, fiber 3 g, protein 25 g, fat 15 g, sodium 149 mg, sugar 3 g*

## *Cilantro Chutney*

MAKES ABOUT 1¼ CUPS

1 large bunch cilantro, tough stems removed

½ yellow bell pepper, seeded and chopped

¼ cup chopped fresh mint

3 tablespoons chopped fresh coconut

1 teaspoon chopped seeded hot green chile, or to taste

½ teaspoon chopped ginger root

1 tablespoon freshly squeezed lemon juice

1 teaspoon ground toasted cumin

Salt

Combine the cilantro, bell pepper, mint, coconut, chile, and ginger in the bowl of a food processor fitted with the metal blade. Process, using quick on and off turns, until finely chopped.

Scrape the mixture into a serving bowl. Add the lemon juice, cumin, and salt to taste and stir to combine. Serve immediately, or cover and store in the refrigerator for up to 1 day.

*Nutritional Analysis per Serving (1 tablespoon): calories 7, carbohydrates 1 g, fiber 0 g, protein 0 g, fat 0 g, sodium 61 mg, sugar 0 g*

# Chicken with Lemon and Olives

SERVES 4

Although I use a quartered chicken, you can cook an assortment of bone-in chicken pieces, Cornish hens, or pork chops in this style. The sauce that results during baking is sweet, sour, and salty—a perfect accent to the mild chicken. Do note that the lemons become quite tender and mellow as they cook, so they should be eaten along with the meat. Thin-skinned organic lemons can be substituted if Meyers are unavailable.

---

1 (3½-pound) chicken, quartered

⅓ cup extra-virgin olive oil

¼ cup dry white wine

2 Meyer lemons, quartered

1 cup kalamata olives

2 tablespoons chopped fresh mint

1 tablespoon chopped fresh thyme

1 tablespoon chopped fresh sage

Salt and pepper

---

Preheat the oven to 400°F.

Place the chicken in a large baking dish and pour in the olive oil and wine. Nestle the lemons around the chicken. Then, sprinkle the olives, mint, thyme, and sage over all. Season with salt and pepper to taste, noting that the olives will add some saltiness to the mix.

Cover and transfer to the preheated oven. Roast for 30 minutes; then, lower the temperature to 350°F and continue to roast until the chicken is golden brown and cooked through, about 20 minutes more.

Remove from the oven and transfer the chicken to a serving platter. Spoon the lemons and olives around the chicken and pour the pan sauce into a gravy boat. Serve hot or at room temperature.

*Nutritional Analysis per Serving: calories 661, carbohydrates 3 g, fiber 1 g, protein 52 g, fat 47 g, sodium 629 mg, sugar 0 g*

# Sesame Chicken

SERVES 4

In place of the expected coating of breadcrumbs or flour, sesame seeds create an amazingly crisp crust for these pan-fried chicken cutlets. The butter-lemon quick sauce isn't necessary, but it adds a little zip to the finished dish. For extra zest, add some minced garlic or ginger to the melting butter.

8 thin chicken cutlets (about 1¼ pounds total)

Salt and pepper

1½ cups sesame seeds

3 tablespoons avocado oil

⅓ cup unsalted butter

Juice of 1 lemon

Season the chicken with salt and pepper to taste.

Place the sesame seeds in a large shallow bowl. Working with one piece at a time, carefully coat both sides of the chicken cutlets with sesame seeds, pressing them to adhere.

Heat the oil in a large frying pan over medium heat. Add the cutlets and fry, turning once, until golden brown and cooked through, about 8 minutes. Transfer the cutlets to a serving platter.

Wipe the oil from the pan and return the pan to medium heat. Add the butter and swirl it around to melt. Stir in the lemon juice and, when combined, pour the sauce over the chicken. Serve immediately.

*Nutritional Analysis per Serving: calories 697, carbohydrates 5 g, fiber 2 g, protein 42 g, fat 57 g, sodium 381 mg, sugar 0 g*

# Herb-Roasted Turkey Breast

SERVES 6

Although terrific on the dinner table, this turkey breast is perfect for out-of-hand snacking at any time of the day. The herb coating adds just the right amount of zesty flavor to the meat. If you are used to supermarket turkey, you can expect heritage turkey to have deeper flavor and darker meat.

¼ cup unsalted butter, at room temperature

1 (3- to 3½-pound) bone-in turkey breast half

½ cup chopped mixed fresh herbs, such as flat-leaf parsley, tarragon, chives, and basil

Salt and pepper

1 cup chicken stock (page 33) or low-sodium chicken broth

Preheat the oven to 425°F.

Using your hands, rub the butter all over the turkey skin. Place the herbs on a clean, flat surface and roll the buttered side of the turkey on them to completely coat the skin. Season with salt and pepper to taste.

Place the seasoned turkey breast in a small roasting pan. Add the stock to the pan and place in the preheated oven.

Roast until an instant-read thermometer inserted into the thickest part registers 160°F, about 30 minutes. Remove from the oven and let rest for about 10 minutes. Cut crosswise into slices and serve with the pan juices drizzled over the top.

*Nutritional Analysis per Serving: calories 214, carbohydrates 1 g, fiber 0 g, protein 32 g, fat 8 g, sodium 456 mg, sugar 0 g*

# Turkey Cutlets with Roasted Peppers and Pepper Jack Cheese

SERVES 4

This dish takes no time and little effort to put together, but it is nonetheless delicious. The combination of textures and flavors takes this dish far, far away from the standard Thanksgiving bird. If you don't have homemade tapenade on hand—which you should—a commercially prepared version will work just fine.

---

4 (4-ounce) turkey cutlets

1 tablespoon avocado oil

Salt and pepper

4 roasted red bell pepper halves

¼ cup Tapenade (page 45)

4 ounces shredded pepper Jack cheese

---

Preheat the broiler, and preheat a stovetop grill pan over medium-high heat.

Generously rub the cutlets with the avocado oil and season with salt and pepper to taste. Place the cutlets in the stovetop grill pan and grill, turning occasionally, until cooked through and nicely marked, about 8 minutes.

Remove the cutlets from the grill pan and place on a small rimmed baking sheet. Lay one roasted pepper half on top of each cutlet. Drizzle a little tapenade over the top and then generously cover with the cheese.

Place under the preheated broiler and broil until the cheese has melted and is bubbly and lightly colored, about 3 minutes. Remove from the oven and serve.

*Nutritional Analysis per Serving: calories 333, carbohydrates 6 g, fiber 2 g, protein 36 g, fat 18 g, sodium 622 mg, sugar 3 g*

# Spicy Turkey Meatballs in Tomato Sauce

SERVES 4

These meatballs are scented with two Italian favorites, basil and cheese, but you can easily change their flavor by substituting herbs and/or spices that reflect other cultures. If you are not a fan of heat, just eliminate the cayenne and you will still have very tasty meatballs. Whatever you do, just remember to match the flavors of the tomato sauce to the flavors of the meat.

1 pound ground dark-meat turkey

¼ cup grated Pecorino Romano cheese

¼ cup minced onion

1 tablespoon chopped fresh flat-leaf parsley

3 tablespoons chopped fresh basil or 1½ teaspoons dried basil

Salt

Cayenne pepper

1 large egg, beaten

3 tablespoons extra-virgin olive oil

1 tablespoon minced garlic

1 (28-ounce) can crushed tomatoes

Black pepper

Red pepper flakes, optional

Combine the ground turkey, grated cheese, onion, and parsley in a large mixing bowl. Add 1 tablespoon of the fresh basil (or ½ teaspoon of the dried basil) along with salt and cayenne to taste. Add the egg and use your hands to thoroughly blend the mixture. Form the turkey into balls about 1 inch in diameter.

Heat 2 tablespoons of the oil in a large frying pan over medium-high heat. Add the meatballs and fry, turning frequently, until nicely browned and cooked through, about 10 minutes. Remove the meatballs from the pan and place on a double layer of paper towels to drain.

Heat the remaining 1 tablespoon oil in a large nonreactive saucepan over medium heat. Add the garlic and cook, stirring, just until slightly softened, about 2 minutes. Add the tomatoes and the remaining 2 tablespoons fresh basil (or 1 teaspoon dried basil). Season with salt and black pepper to taste and, if using, red pepper flakes.

Add the meatballs and bring to a simmer. Lower the heat and cook at a gentle simmer for 15 minutes. Serve immediately.

**VARIATIONS:** These meatballs can be made with ground chicken, pork, or beef.

*Nutritional Analysis per Serving: calories 489, carbohydrates 17 g, fiber 5 g, protein 34 g, fat 32 g, sodium 580 mg, sugar 5 g*

# Fish and Shellfish

_____

# Salmon Roasted in Butter and Almonds

SERVES 4

Salmon, butter, and almonds—what could be better? If you can, do garnish with the cracked pepper. It offers just a hint of heat to balance the fatty fish and the buttery sauce.

---

1 (1½-pound) skin-on salmon fillet

Salt and pepper

6 tablespoons unsalted butter

¾ cup slivered almonds

1 tablespoon freshly squeezed lemon juice

2 tablespoons chopped fresh chives

Cracked black pepper, for optional garnish

---

Preheat the oven to 500°F.

Season the salmon with salt and pepper to taste. Set aside.

Place the butter and almonds in a small baking pan in the preheated oven. When the butter has melted, add the salmon, flesh-side down. Roast for 5 minutes; then, turn and continue to roast until the salmon is barely beginning to flake, about 3 minutes more. (You can test by sticking the point of a small, sharp knife into the flesh to see if it flakes or easily comes apart.)

Remove the pan from the oven and transfer the salmon to a serving platter. Stir the lemon juice and chives into the "sauce" in the pan and immediately pour over the salmon. Sprinkle with cracked black pepper, if desired, and serve.

*Nutritional Analysis per Serving: calories 602, carbohydrates 5 g, fiber 3 g, protein 42 g, fat 46 g, sodium 377 mg, sugar 1 g*

# Salmon in Chile Broth

SERVES 4

This is a light dish to serve any time of the year. If you are not a fan of salmon—or have had too many salmon dinners this month—use any other meaty fish you like; halibut or grouper would make a more than acceptable substitute.

---

2 cups bottled clam juice

1 small hot green chile, seeded and thinly sliced crosswise

2 teaspoons anchovy paste

1 teaspoon tahini

1 teaspoon freshly squeezed lime juice

1 teaspoon ginger root slivers

4 (6-ounce) skin-on salmon fillets

1 teaspoon almond oil

Salt

2 cups tiny broccoli florets

1 tablespoon chopped fresh chives

1 teaspoon black sesame seeds, optional

---

Preheat the oven to 375°F.

Combine the clam juice, chile, anchovy paste, tahini, lime juice, and ginger in a medium saucepan over medium heat. Cover and bring to a simmer. Simmer just long enough to allow the flavors to blend, about 5 minutes. Uncover and turn off the heat, but leave the pan on the stove.

Lightly brush the salmon with the oil and season with salt to taste. Place the fish, skin-side down, in an oven-safe frying pan over high heat. Sear just until the skin is crisp and the salmon has begun to cook, about 4 minutes.

Turn the salmon over and transfer the pan to the preheated oven. Bake until the fish barely flakes with a fork, about 4 minutes.

While the fish is in the oven, add the broccoli to the broth and cook over medium heat until crisp-tender but still bright green, about 3 minutes.

Ladle an equal portion of the broth and broccoli into each of four shallow soups bowls.

Remove the fish from the oven and use a spatula to place one fillet in the center of each bowl. Sprinkle all over with the chives and black sesame seeds (if using) and serve.

*Nutritional Analysis per Serving: calories 237, carbohydrates 3 g, fiber 1 g, protein 36 g, fat 8 g, sodium 681 mg, sugar 1 g*

# Salmon Burgers with Herbed Tartar Sauce

SERVES 4

A bit more interesting than old-fashioned salmon croquettes, these burgers would make an inviting party dish served on a bed of sautéed greens. You don't absolutely need the tartar sauce, but it adds that little touch of sour that complements the richness of the salmon.

---

1 pound fresh salmon, chopped

1 large egg yolk

¼ cup finely diced red or yellow bell pepper

¼ cup almond meal

2 tablespoons Dijon mustard

1 tablespoon chopped fresh chives

Salt and white pepper

1 tablespoon clarified butter (see page 42), ghee, or unsalted butter, melted

½ cup Herbed Tartar Sauce (recipe follows)

---

Preheat and oil the grill or preheat a stovetop grill pan over medium-high heat.

Combine the salmon, egg yolk, bell pepper, almond meal, mustard, and chives in a large mixing bowl. Season with salt and white pepper to taste. Use your hands to form the mixture into 4 patties of equal size.

Using a pastry brush, coat both sides of the patties with the clarified butter. Place on the grill (or stovetop grill pan) and grill for 4 minutes. Turn and grill until cooked through, about 5 minutes more. Remove from the heat and serve, with the tartar sauce on the side.

*Nutritional Analysis per Serving (includes 2 tablespoons tartar sauce): calories 284, carbohydrates 5 g, fiber 1 g, protein 25 g, fat 18 g, sodium 481 mg, sugar 1 g*

# Herbed Tartar Sauce

MAKES ABOUT 1 CUP

---

3 green olives

1 shallot, chopped

1 large hard-boiled egg yolk

¼ cup cornichons (see Note)

1 teaspoon chopped capers

1 teaspoon chopped fresh flat-leaf parsley

1 teaspoon chopped fresh chives

1 teaspoon chopped fresh dill

½ cup Mayonnaise (page 40)

1 teaspoon Dijon mustard

Salt and pepper

---

Combine the olives, shallot, egg yolk, cornichons, capers, parsley, chives, and dill in the bowl of a food processor fitted with the metal blade. Process, using quick on and off turns, until coarsely chopped—you do not want a puree. Add the mayonnaise and mustard and process to blend. Taste and season with salt and pepper to taste.

Scrape the tartar sauce from the processor bowl into a clean container, cover, and store in the refrigerator until ready to use, up to 3 days.

**NOTE:** Cornichons are small French pickles that are often known in this country as gherkins. They are available from specialty food stores, many supermarkets, or online.

*Nutritional Analysis per Serving (2 tablespoons): calories 55, carbohydrates 1 g, fiber 0 g, protein 0 g, fat 6 g, sodium 95 mg, sugar 0 g*

# Slow-Roasted Salmon with Mustard Glaze

SERVES 4

Slowly roasting this dish gives the buttery glaze time to shine and allows the salmon to remain moist and flavorful. The heat of the mustard is the perfect balance for the sweet, fatty fish. A side of a peppery watercress salad or Green Beans with Walnuts (page 162) would complete the meal.

---

6 tablespoons unsalted butter, at room temperature, plus more for greasing the pan

¼ cup finely ground raw almonds

2 tablespoons chopped fresh flat-leaf parsley

2 teaspoons Dijon mustard

1 teaspoon mustard seeds

1 teaspoon freshly grated lemon zest

4 (5-ounce) skinless salmon fillets

Salt and pepper

---

Preheat the oven to 275°F. Generously butter a shallow baking dish large enough to hold the fish without crowding.

Place the butter in a small mixing bowl. Add the almonds, parsley, mustard, mustard seeds, and lemon zest and use a rubber spatula to knead and blend thoroughly.

Spread an equal portion of the butter mixture over the top of each salmon fillet. Season with salt and pepper to taste and then transfer to the roasting pan.

Place in the preheated oven and roast just until the fish is barely cooked through and the top is glazed, about 20 minutes. Remove from the oven and serve.

*Nutritional Analysis per Serving: calories 313, carbohydrates 2 g, fiber 1 g, protein 30 g, fat 20 g, sodium 279 mg, sugar 0 g*

# Mint-Coconut Salmon

The barely cooked slaw is the perfect accent to the moist, coconut-flavored salmon. Combining the vegetables and the protein in one package helps bring dinner to the table in a snap. The extra benefit is that the packets can be put together a couple of hours in advance of cooking and popped into the oven at the last minute for a stress-free meal.

---

1 cup shredded green cabbage

¼ cup finely diced red bell pepper

1 tablespoon shredded unsweetened coconut

1 tablespoon chopped fresh mint, plus more for garnish

2 teaspoons chopped fresh cilantro

1 teaspoon freshly squeezed lime juice

Salt and pepper

4 (5-ounce) salmon fillets

⅓ cup unsweetened coconut milk

2 tablespoons toasted coconut flakes, for garnish

---

Preheat the oven to 350°F. Cut four pieces of parchment paper into a heart shape, each about 12 inches long. Set aside.

In a mixing bowl, toss the cabbage with the bell pepper, coconut, mint, cilantro, and lime juice. Season with salt and pepper to taste.

Place one-quarter of the seasoned cabbage on one side of each heart shape, near the center. Season the fish with salt and pepper to taste and then lay a piece on top of the cabbage in each packet. Drizzle coconut milk over the top and fold the other side of the paper up and over the salmon so the two sides meet. Starting at one end of the half heart, begin folding the edges in and over to make a tightly crimped seal as you work your way around to firmly enclose the cabbage and salmon. If desired, you can wet the inner edge of the paper with a bit of egg white before folding it over the salmon to ensure a tight seal.

Place the packets in a baking pan in the preheated oven and bake for 12 minutes.

Place a packet on each of four dinner plates, to be opened at the table. Garnish each fillet with a sprinkle of toasted coconut and chopped mint leaves and serve.

*Nutritional Analysis per Serving: calories 247, carbohydrates 5 g, fiber 2 g, protein 29 g, fat 12 g, sodium 229 mg, sugar 2 g*

# Herb-Grilled Halibut Steaks

SERVES 4

Fresh herbs make all the difference in this recipe, giving a lighter, cleaner flavor than dried. However, if you don't have them on hand, don't hesitate to replace them with dried herbs—just remember that you will require substantially less, as the flavor of the dried herbs is more intense. The herb-crusted fish looks absolutely delectable served with Healthy Green Slaw (page 130), Radishes Braised in Butter (page 145), or Sautéed Cherry Tomatoes in Herbs (page 149).

¼ cup chopped fresh thyme

¼ cup chopped fresh oregano

¼ cup chopped fresh flat-leaf parsley

Cayenne pepper

Salt and black pepper

¼ cup coconut oil

4 (5-ounce) halibut steaks (about ¾ inch thick)

Preheat and oil the grill or preheat a stovetop grill pan over medium-high heat.

Combine the thyme, oregano, and parsley in a shallow bowl. Season with cayenne, salt, and black pepper to taste, tossing to blend well.

Using a pastry brush, generously coat both sides of the halibut steaks with the coconut oil. Press both sides of the fish into the herb mixture, pushing down to coat well.

Place the steaks on the preheated grill (or stovetop grill pan). Grill, turning once, until the fish is just barely cooked through, about 12 minutes. Remove from the heat and serve.

*Nutritional Analysis per Serving: calories 413, carbohydrates 2 g, fiber 1 g, protein 22 g, fat 35 g, sodium 415 mg, sugar 0 g*

# Grilled Brook Trout with Brown Butter

SERVES 4

Effortless and classic—what more could a cook want? This is a piece of cake to put together and always makes a strong impression. You can, if you wish, add about ¼ cup slivered almonds to the butter as it is browning for an extra *Grain Brain* hit.

---

½ cup unsalted butter

1 teaspoon freshly squeezed lemon juice

1 tablespoon chopped fresh flat-leaf parsley

1 teaspoon chopped fresh chives

Salt and white pepper

4 whole trout, cleaned

---

Melt the butter in a small frying pan over low heat. Cook, stirring frequently, until it begins to foam, about 3 minutes. Continue to cook slowly until it turns golden brown and the aroma is very nutty, taking care that it doesn't burn. Remove from the heat and stir in the lemon juice, parsley, and chives. Season with salt and white pepper to taste. Set aside and cover to keep warm while the fish grills.

Preheat and oil the grill or preheat a stovetop grill pan over medium-high heat.

Season the trout with salt and white pepper to taste. Place on the preheated grill (or stovetop grill pan) and grill for 4 minutes. Carefully turn (preferably with a fish spatula) to keep the fish whole, and grill until cooked through, about 5 minutes more. Remove from the grill and serve, with the brown butter drizzled over the top.

*Nutritional Analysis per Serving: calories 450, carbohydrates 0 g, fiber 0 g, protein 35 g, fat 33 g, sodium 378 mg, sugar 0 g*

# Whole Roasted Red Snapper

SERVES 4

There's nothing like a fresh-from-the-ocean whole fish cooked simply. You can roast the fish in a hot oven or do a quick turn on the grill—either way it is deliciously moist. This recipe can be used for almost any firm-fleshed fish or thick fillets of meaty fish such as halibut. Roasting whole fish at a high temperature seals in its juices so it remains extremely moist.

---

2 (2½- to 3-pound) red snapper, cleaned, head and tail intact

1 lemon, cut crosswise into thin slices, plus more for optional garnish

8 dill sprigs, plus chopped dill for optional garnish

8 flat-leaf parsley sprigs, plus chopped parsley for optional garnish

3 tablespoons avocado oil

Salt and pepper

2 large fennel bulbs, cut crosswise into thin slices

2 onions, cut crosswise into thin slices

2 tablespoons chopped fennel fronds

½ cup water

---

Preheat the oven to 450°F.

Rinse the fish and pat dry, both inside and out. Layer half of the lemon slices in the cavity of each fish. Place 4 sprigs each of dill and parsley in each cavity. Using your hands, generously coat the fish with the oil and season both sides with salt and pepper.

Combine the fennel and onion slices with the chopped fennel fronds in a large, shallow roasting pan. Season with salt and pepper to taste and spread out the vegetables in an even layer. Pour the water into the pan and place the fish on top of the vegetables.

Place in the preheated oven and roast, turning the vegetables occasionally, until the vegetables are tender and an instant-read thermometer inserted into the thickest part of the fish reads 135°F, about 30 minutes. Remove the pan from the oven and allow the fish to rest for 5 minutes.

Using two spatulas, carefully lift each fish from the roasting pan onto a serving platter. Spoon the fennel-onion mixture around the fish and, if desired, garnish with chopped dill or parsley and additional lemon slices. Serve.

*Nutritional Analysis per Serving: calories 289, carbohydrates 7 g, fiber 2 g, protein 35 g, fat 13 g, sodium 392 mg, sugar 4 g*

# Ginger-Glazed Mahimahi

SERVES 4

The key to this recipe is to bake the fish in a very hot oven, which both cooks the fish quickly and creates an attractive glazed coating. If you can't find lemongrass, replace it with about a teaspoon of freshly grated lemon zest. The flavor will be a bit more intense, but it will still be delicious. A notable partner for the mahimahi would be the Jicama-Cucumber Relish on page 216.

2 lemongrass stalks (white parts only), chopped

2 tablespoons finely chopped fresh cilantro

1 tablespoon grated ginger root

1 tablespoon coconut oil

1 tablespoon white balsamic vinegar

Salt and pepper

4 (5-ounce) mahimahi fillets

Preheat the oven to 450°F.

Combine the lemongrass, cilantro, ginger, coconut oil, vinegar, and salt and pepper to taste in a small mixing bowl. Using your fingertips, spread the mixture over one side of each fish fillet and set aside to marinate for 10 minutes.

Place the fish in a nonstick oven-safe pan, coated-side up. Transfer to the preheated oven and roast just until the fish is barely cooked and the coating has glazed, about 5 minutes. Remove from the oven and serve.

*Nutritional Analysis per Serving: calories 191, carbohydrates 2 g, fiber 0 g, protein 34 g, fat 5 g, sodium 307 mg, sugar 1 g*

# Fillet of Sole in Champagne Sauce

SERVES 4

This classic French dish was once very popular in four-star restaurants but is rarely seen anymore. It is quick to put together and delicious, and it makes a stunning presentation when served in individual gratin dishes at the table.

---

½ cup plus 3 tablespoons unsalted butter, at room temperature

½ cup chicken stock (page 33) or low-sodium chicken broth

¼ cup bottled clam juice

4 (4-ounce) sole fillets or other delicate white fish fillets

8 ounces small shrimp, peeled and deveined

12 shucked oysters, well drained

¼ cup champagne or other sparkling white wine

4 large egg yolks, beaten, at room temperature

Salt and white pepper

1 tablespoon chopped fresh chives, for garnish

---

Preheat the oven to 325°F. Using 3 tablespoons of the butter, generously coat the interior of a shallow baking dish large enough to hold the fish, or four individual gratin dishes.

Combine the chicken stock and clam juice. Set aside.

Arrange the fish fillets in a single layer in the baking dish. Pour ¼ cup of the clam juice–chicken stock mixture over the top. Place the shrimp and oysters on top of the fish. Cover the dish tightly with aluminum foil without allowing the foil to touch the fish.

Place in the preheated oven and bake just until the fish is cooked through, about 15 minutes.

While the fish is cooking, place the remaining ½ cup clam juice–chicken stock mixture in the top half of a double boiler placed over high heat. Bring to a boil and boil until reduced by half, about 7 minutes. Meanwhile, bring a few inches of water to a boil in the bottom half of the double boiler set over high heat.

When the clam juice–chicken stock mixture is reduced, place the top half of the double boiler over the bottom half. Whisk in the champagne and, when hot, whisk in the remaining ½ cup butter until emulsified.

Place the egg yolks in a small mixing bowl. Whisking constantly, beat about ¼ cup of the hot mixture into the yolks until well blended. Beating constantly, add the tempered egg yolks to the hot mixture in the top of the double boiler. Return the entire double boiler to high heat, season the sauce with salt and white pepper to taste, and continue to cook, whisking constantly, until the sauce is smooth and thick, about 5 minutes.

Remove the fish from the oven and turn the oven temperature to broil.

Uncover the fish and pour the sauce over the top. Place under the broiler and broil until bubbling and golden brown, about 3 minutes. Remove from the oven, sprinkle with the chopped chives, and serve.

*Nutritional Analysis per Serving: calories 492, carbohydrates 4 g, fiber 0 g, protein 27 g, fat 39 g, sodium 815 mg, sugar 0 g*

# Portuguese-Style Sardines

SERVES 4

Only in recent years have fresh sardines been available in America, after nutritionists began promoting their health benefits. Unlike many other fish, sardines still seem to be abundant. They are rich in protein, offer one of the most concentrated sources of the omega-3 fatty acids EPA and DHA, contain plenty of vitamins $B_{12}$ and D, and taste delicious. They can be cooked simply on the grill and served with just a squeeze of lemon, with any number of sauces, or in this delightful Portuguese-style recipe.

---

4 tablespoons extra-virgin olive oil

8 large sardines, cleaned

1 medium onion, cut lengthwise into slivers

1 tablespoon minced garlic

1 red bell pepper, seeded and cut lengthwise into thin slices

3 cups diced very ripe tomatoes, with their juice

1 bay leaf

½ teaspoon saffron

4 oil-packed anchovies, drained and chopped

---

Preheat the oven to 400°F. Using 1 tablespoon of the oil, generously coat the interior of a baking dish large enough to hold the fish in a single layer. Place the fish in the dish and set aside.

Heat the remaining 3 tablespoons oil in a large frying pan over medium heat. Add the onion and garlic and cook, stirring occasionally, for 5 minutes. Add the bell pepper and continue to cook, stirring occasionally, until the onion and pepper are nicely colored, about 6 minutes more.

Stir in the tomatoes, along with the bay leaf and saffron. Bring to a simmer and simmer for 5 minutes. Then, pour the tomato mixture over the fish and season with salt and pepper to taste. Dot the top of the fish with the chopped anchovies.

Transfer to the preheated oven and bake until the fish is cooked through and the sauce aromatic, about 20 minutes. Remove from the oven and serve hot or at room temperature.

*Nutritional Analysis per Serving: calories 410, carbohydrates 10 g, fiber 3 g, protein 31 g, fat 28 g, sodium 446 mg, sugar 6 g*

# Garlic Shrimp

SERVES 4

This is my version of a dish that on Italian menus is known as "scampi." It is usually served with lots of bread, but I think it more than stands on its own. Like almost every protein, scampi works well with a side of sautéed greens. Cook the shrimp very briefly or you'll have chewy little monsters.

---

6 tablespoons clarified butter (see page 42), ghee, or unsalted butter

¼ cup finely chopped garlic

¼ cup dry white wine

3 tablespoons freshly squeezed lemon juice

1 pound large shrimp, peeled and deveined

Salt and pepper

2 tablespoons minced fresh flat-leaf parsley

---

Heat the butter in a large frying pan over medium heat. Add the garlic and cook, stirring, just until soft but not colored, about 2 minutes.

Stir in the wine and lemon juice and, when blended, add the shrimp. Season with salt and pepper to taste and bring to a simmer. Simmer just until the shrimp are firm and pink, about 2 minutes. Do not overcook or the shrimp will be tough.

Remove from the heat and stir in the parsley. Serve immediately.

**NOTE:** For those on a restricted sodium diet, just be aware that shrimp on its own is quite high in sodium, so you might want to substitute chunks of a firm white fish in its place.

*Nutritional Analysis per Serving: calories 281, carbohydrates 5 g, fiber 0 g, protein 20 g, fat 18 g, sodium 819 mg, sugar 0 g*

# Shrimp Creole

This recipe will take you down on the bayou with just a few minutes in the kitchen. If you don't have Creole seasoning on hand, you can make your own by combining 2 tablespoons each salt, paprika, and cayenne pepper with 1 tablespoon each dried thyme, dried oregano, onion powder, garlic powder, and black pepper.

---

2 tablespoons extra-virgin olive oil

1 cup diced onion

½ cup finely diced red bell pepper

½ cup finely diced green bell pepper

1 tablespoon minced garlic

1 tablespoon Creole seasoning

1 tablespoon tomato paste

2 cups fresh or canned diced tomatoes, drained

1 cup bottled clam juice

Pepper

1 pound large shrimp, peeled and deveined

1 tablespoon chopped fresh flat-leaf parsley

---

Heat the oil in a large frying pan over medium heat. Add the onion, bell peppers, and garlic and cook, stirring frequently, until the vegetables begin to soften, about 5 minutes. Stir in the Creole seasoning and tomato paste and cook for another minute. Add the tomatoes and clam juice and bring to a simmer. Taste and, if necessary, add pepper.

Simmer until the flavors are well blended, about 20 minutes. Add the shrimp and return to the simmer. Cook just until the shrimp are firm and pink, about 3 minutes. Do not overcook or the shrimp will be tough.

Remove from the heat, stir in the parsley, and serve.

*Nutritional Analysis per Serving: calories 202, carbohydrates 10 g, fiber 2 g, protein 21 g, fat 9 g, sodium 892 mg, sugar 4 g*

# Cioppino

Cioppino is a traditional San Francisco shellfish stew created by early Italian settlers who fished the local waters. It is similar to all Mediterranean fish stews in that you can make it with almost any combination of fish and shellfish and in any base, although tomato is almost always the defining flavor. This recipe uses only shellfish, but you can easily replace some or most of the shellfish with finfish. It is up to you to make it everything you want an aromatic stew to be.

½ cup extra-virgin olive oil

4 large garlic cloves, sliced

1 large onion, chopped

1 carrot, peeled and minced

1 fennel bulb, cut lengthwise into thin slices

½ cup dry red wine

2 (28-ounce) cans diced Italian plum tomatoes, with their juice

1 cup bottled clam juice

2 tablespoons chopped fresh basil

2 tablespoons chopped fresh flat-leaf parsley, plus more for optional garnish

Salt and pepper

1 or 2 Dungeness crabs, cracked into pieces

24 clams

24 mussels

Heat the olive oil in a large stockpot over medium heat. Add the garlic, onion, carrot, and fennel and cook, stirring frequently, until the vegetables begin to soften, about 5 minutes. Add the wine and cook until most of the alcohol has burned off, about 5 minutes.

Stir in the tomatoes and the clam juice and bring to a simmer. Stir in the basil and parsley and season with salt and pepper to taste. Cook at a low simmer until the flavors have blended nicely, about 15 minutes.

Add the crab pieces, clams, and mussels. Cover and cook until the shellfish is cooked and the shells have opened, about 10 minutes.

Ladle the stew into individual shallow soup bowls or one large soup tureen. Garnish with additional parsley, if desired, and serve.

*Nutritional Analysis per Serving: calories 425, carbohydrates 23 g, fiber 5 g, protein 33 g, fat 22 g, sodium 821 mg, sugar 9 g*

# Meatless

---

# Baked Eggplant, Zucchini, and Tomato

SERVES 4

This all-year-round casserole sings of the South of France and hints at a touch of Italy. It can be made early in the day and baked just before dinner. It is terrific at room temperature, too, which makes leftovers perfect for lunch the next day.

---

¼ cup extra-virgin olive oil, plus more for greasing the pan

1 large eggplant, halved lengthwise and then cut crosswise into ¼-inch-thick slices

4 zucchini, cut lengthwise into ¼-inch-thick slices

Salt and pepper

½ cup Tomato Sauce (page 39)

5 ripe tomatoes, peeled, cored, and cut crosswise into thin slices

¼ cup torn basil leaves

12 ounces shredded mozzarella cheese

¼ cup grated Parmesan cheese

---

Preheat the oven to 450°F. Line two baking sheets with parchment paper and set aside. Lightly coat the interior of an 8-inch square baking pan with olive oil and set aside.

Using a pastry brush, lightly coat both sides of the eggplant and zucchini with olive oil. Place the vegetables on the prepared baking sheets and season with salt and pepper to taste. Place in the preheated oven and bake until just barely cooked and lightly browned, about 12 minutes. Remove from the oven and set aside to cool.

Lower the oven temperature to 350°F.

Ladle the tomato sauce into the prepared baking dish. Using half of the eggplant slices, place a layer of eggplant over the sauce. Top the eggplant with half of the zucchini slices, laying them in the opposite direction from the eggplant. Cover the zucchini with half of the tomato slices. Sprinkle half of the basil over the tomatoes and season with salt and pepper to taste. Then sprinkle half of the mozzarella over the seasoned tomatoes, making an even layer. Repeat the layers, beginning with the remaining eggplant and ending with the remaining mozzarella. Sprinkle the top with the Parmesan and transfer to the preheated oven.

Bake until hot throughout and the cheese has melted and browned slightly, about 30 minutes. Remove from the oven and let rest for 10 minutes before cutting into squares and serving.

*Nutritional Analysis per Serving: calories 538, carbohydrates 25 g, fiber 7 g, protein 26 g, fat 40 g, sodium 559 mg, sugar 13 g*

# Chiles Stuffed with Goat Cheese

SERVES 4

It takes a little work to make these chiles, but the time and effort are well worth the result. Not at all spicy, stuffed chiles are wonderfully delicious and deserve to be on the table frequently. If you can't find the chiles called for in the recipe, you can use almost any other chile, including ordinary green bell peppers.

---

4 roasted red bell peppers, seeded

2 tablespoons extra-virgin olive oil

1 teaspoon balsamic vinegar

1½ teaspoons ground toasted cumin

½ teaspoon Tabasco sauce, or to taste

Salt

4 fresh New Mexico green chiles or Anaheim chiles

4 ounces mild goat cheese

1 ounce pepper Jack cheese

¼ cup chopped oil-packed sun-dried tomatoes, well drained

3 large eggs, separated

¼ cup coconut oil, for frying

---

Preheat the broiler.

Combine the roasted bell peppers with the oil and vinegar in the bowl of a food processor fitted with the metal blade. Add 1 teaspoon of the cumin and process to a smooth puree. Scrape into a mixing bowl and season with the Tabasco and salt to taste. Cover and set aside.

Place the chiles on a broiler pan under the hot broiler and broil, turning occasionally, until nicely charred but not completely blackened, about 7 minutes. Remove from the oven and immediately place in a resealable plastic bag or a container with a tight lid. Seal or cover and allow to sweat until the skin has begun to loosen from the flesh, about 15 minutes.

Remove the chiles and, working with one at a time, gently push off the charred skin, taking care not to tear the chiles. Using a small, sharp knife, slit each chile lengthwise down one side. Carefully pull back the flesh and remove and discard the seeds. Set aside.

Combine the goat cheese, Jack cheese, sun-dried tomatoes, and remaining ½ teaspoon cumin in the bowl of a food processor fitted with the metal blade and process until smooth.

Place the chiles on a clean, flat work surface and carefully spoon one-quarter of the cheese mixture into the opening of each, using just enough cheese to fill the cavity yet still allow the chile to close around it. Use your fingers to lightly press the edges of the chile together.

Place the egg yolks in a medium mixing bowl. Add ¼ teaspoon salt and whisk until light.

Place the whites in the bowl of a standing electric mixer and beat on high until stiff peaks form. Remove the bowl from the mixer and slowly fold the beaten egg yolks into the whites. Continue folding until only a few lines of egg yolk are evident.

Heat the oil in a large, deep frying pan over medium-high heat until shimmering but not smoking.

Working with one chile at a time, carefully dip the chile into the beaten eggs. This is most easily done by holding the chile on a large perforated spatula and dipping it in and out of the egg. Do not press on the chile or the stuffing will pop out.

Carefully lay the chiles in the hot oil and fry, turning once, until the coating is golden brown and slightly crisp, about 4 minutes. Remove from the oil and place on a double layer of paper towels to drain briefly.

Ladle about ⅓ cup of the roasted red pepper sauce onto the center of each of four serving plates. Lay a stuffed chile in the center and serve immediately, as the chiles will get soggy quickly.

*Nutritional Analysis per Serving: calories 316, carbohydrates 15 g, fiber 4 g, protein 14 g, fat 24 g, sodium 285 mg, sugar 10 g*

# Baked Spaghetti Squash with Tomato Sauce and Parmesan Cheese

SERVES 4

Spaghetti squash really can take the place of wheat-based pasta. Once you get the hang of roasting it and pulling the flesh out in strands, you will see what I mean. You can use it with any type of sauce that you would normally use for pasta; even the classic Italian *cacio e pepe* (cheese and peppers) would make a sublime meal.

Since this dish is relatively high in carbohydrates, take care about the remainder of your total carbohydrate intake for the day.

---

1 tablespoon plus 1 teaspoon extra-virgin olive oil, plus more for greasing the pan

1 (5-pound) spaghetti squash

¼ cup water

4 cups coarsely chopped button mushrooms

1 small onion, chopped

1 teaspoon minced garlic

1 recipe Tomato Sauce (page 39)

Salt and pepper

1 tablespoon chopped fresh basil

½ cup grated Parmesan cheese

---

Preheat the oven to 375°F. Lightly coat the interior of an 8-inch square baking pan with olive oil and set aside.

Cut the squash in half lengthwise. Using a spoon, carefully scoop out the seeds. Either discard the seeds or set them aside to dry out and roast at a later time (see page 271).

Place the squash, cut-side down, in a 9-by-13-inch baking dish. Add the water and 1 tablespoon of the olive oil to the pan. Transfer to the preheated oven and bake until very tender when pierced with the end of a small, sharp knife, about 30 minutes.

Remove the squash from the oven (do not turn the oven off) and turn it over. Using a kitchen fork, carefully scrape the stringy flesh from the skin in long spaghetti-like strands. Mound the spaghetti squash in the prepared baking pan and set aside.

Heat the remaining 1 teaspoon olive oil in a large frying pan over medium heat. Add the mushrooms, onion, and garlic and cook, stirring, until the mushrooms are nicely browned, about 15 minutes. Add the tomato sauce and continue to cook for 20 minutes. Taste and, if necessary, season with salt and pepper to taste. Stir in the basil and remove from the heat.

Spoon the sauce over the squash. Top with the Parmesan cheese, transfer to the oven, and bake until the top is lightly browned and the squash is very hot, about 15 minutes. Remove from the oven and serve.

*Nutritional Analysis per Serving: calories 336, carbohydrates 44 g, fiber 10 g, protein 13 g, fat 15 g, sodium 615 mg, sugar 18 g*

# Sautéed Summer Squash "Noodles" with Butter and Cheese

SERVES 4

The nutty brown butter and salty cheese turn the mild squash into something supreme—and even better tasting than wheat-based noodles. You do need a julienne vegetable peeler to get the long strands necessary, but they are inexpensive and available at most housewares stores or, of course, online.

---

3 yellow squash (about 1 pound)

3 zucchini (about 1 pound)

½ cup unsalted butter, cut into pieces

Salt and pepper

¾ cup grated Parmesan cheese

1 cup shredded arugula

---

Using a julienne peeler, begin at one end of one squash and pull the peeler all the way down the length of the squash to make long noodle-like strands. Continue making strands until all of the squash and zucchini have been cut.

Place the butter in a large frying pan over medium heat and cook, stirring constantly, until it just begins to brown, about 4 minutes. Add the squash and zucchini strands, season with salt and pepper to taste, and cook, tossing and turning with tongs, until just barely tender and well coated with brown butter.

Remove from the heat and toss in the cheese and arugula. Taste and, if necessary, season with additional salt and pepper. Serve immediately.

*Nutritional Analysis per Serving: calories 350, carbohydrates 7 g, fiber 2 g, protein 12 g, fat 29 g, sodium 674 mg, sugar 5 g*

# SNACKS

———————

A COUPLE OF SNACKS during the day can add diversity to your diet, and any of the options in this section will more than accomplish that. Some of these recipes take no effort, some create enough to see you through the week, some work as a side dish, and some are fabulous special-occasion treats. All of them make outstanding party and entertaining fare and, believe me, your guests will be none the wiser that they have been snacking on "good-for-you" foods.

# Roasted Pumpkin or Squash Seeds

MAKES ABOUT 1 CUP, DEPENDING ON THE SIZE OF YOUR PUMPKIN
OR SQUASH

Waste not, want not, the old saying goes. Many of us throw out the seeds we scrape from hard squashes when they can easily be turned into a healthy and tasty snack food. When baking the seeds, you can add any herb or spice you like—about 1 teaspoon ground spice should be enough to season the seeds from one squash.

Seeds from 1 pumpkin or other winter squash (such as butternut or acorn)

2 tablespoons extra-virgin olive oil, coconut oil, or avocado oil

Salt, optional

Preheat the oven to 300°F. Line a rimmed baking sheet with parchment paper and set aside.

Using your fingertips, clean off any pieces of flesh clinging to the seeds. Place the seeds in a colander under cold running water and rinse thoroughly to remove any stringy pieces of flesh remaining. Transfer the seeds to a double layer of paper towels to drain. Using more paper towels, pat off any water that remains.

Place the seeds on the prepared baking sheet. Add the oil and, if using, salt to taste, tossing to coat. Be sure that the seeds are in a single layer so that they will roast evenly.

Transfer to the preheated oven and roast, stirring occasionally, until the seeds are beginning to turn golden brown, about 25 minutes.

Remove from the oven and serve warm, or set aside to cool completely. Store leftovers in an airtight container at room temperature for up to 5 days.

*Nutritional Analysis per Serving (2 tablespoons): calories 293, carbohydrates 5 g, fiber 1 g, protein 11 g, fat 26 g, sodium 7 mg, sugar 0 g*

# Crunchy Pumpkin Seed Toss

MAKES ABOUT 1 CUP

This zesty seed-nut mixture makes a perfect afternoon snack. You can easily triple the amount of seeds and nuts and still use the same amount of egg whites and spices. This mix also makes a wonderful garnish on vegetables or grilled chicken or fish.

---

½ cup pumpkin seeds

¼ cup raw cashews

¼ cup sunflower seeds

2 tablespoons chia seeds

2 large egg whites, at room temperature

1 teaspoon curry powder

¼ teaspoon cayenne pepper

Pinch ground turmeric

Pinch stevia powder

Salt

---

Preheat the oven to 300°F. Line a rimmed baking sheet with parchment paper and set aside.

Using your fingertips, clean off any pieces of flesh clinging to the pumpkin seeds. Place the seeds in a colander under cold running water and rinse thoroughly to remove any stringy pieces of flesh remaining. Transfer the seeds to a double layer of paper towels to drain. Using more paper towels, pat off any water that remains.

Combine the pumpkin seeds, cashews, sunflower seeds, and chia seeds in a medium mixing bowl.

Place the egg whites in a small mixing bowl. Whisk in the curry powder, cayenne, turmeric, and stevia until very frothy.

Pour the egg white mixture over the seeds and nuts and toss to coat well. Using a slotted spoon, transfer the mixture to the prepared baking sheet, taking care to allow excess egg white to drip off. Transfer to the preheated oven and bake, turning occasionally, until golden brown and crisp, about 30 minutes.

Remove from the oven and season with salt to taste. Let cool before serving. Store leftovers in an airtight container at room temperature for up to 1 week.

*Nutritional Analysis per Serving (2 tablespoons): calories 293, carbohydrates 5 g, fiber 1 g, protein 11 g, fat 26 g, sodium 7 mg, sugar 0 g*

# Kale Chips

SERVES 4

Kale chips didn't exist a couple of years ago, but now you find them in stores all across the country. You can easily make them yourself and have them on hand to snack on throughout the day. (You can, in fact, bake any leafy green in this same fashion.) They are a terrific alternative to commercial chips, potato or otherwise.

---

1 large bunch kale, tough stems removed and leaves cut into large pieces

3 tablespoons extra-virgin olive oil or coconut oil

Salt

---

Preheat the oven to 300°F. Line two rimmed baking sheets with parchment paper and set aside.

Place the kale in a large mixing bowl. Add the oil and salt to taste, and toss to coat well. Spread the kale on the prepared baking sheets in a single layer. Transfer to the preheated oven and bake until the kale begins to brown, about 8 minutes. Using tongs, turn the kale and continue to bake until brown, crisp, and crackly, about 12 minutes more.

Remove from the oven and season with additional salt, if desired. Serve immediately, or cool and store in an airtight container at room temperature for up to 3 days. If the chips lose their crunch, reheat in a 275°F oven for 5 minutes.

*Nutritional Analysis per Serving: calories 132, carbohydrates 8 g, fiber 2 g, protein 4 g, fat 11 g, sodium 178 mg, sugar 0 g*

# Vegetable Chips

Homemade veggie chips are far better for you than commercial potato chips but just as satisfying. Along with salt, you can season them with black pepper, cayenne, ground herbs, and/or spices. You can use one or all of the following vegetables to make chips — it's up to you to create your own variety.

---

1 large beet, peeled

1 celery root, peeled

1 rutabaga, peeled

1 lotus or taro root, peeled

1 pound sunchokes, well scrubbed

1 jicama, peeled

1 large carrot, peeled

Coconut oil, extra-virgin olive oil, or avocado oil, for
  deep-frying

Salt

---

Using a Japanese vegetable slicer or a mandoline, slice the vegetables as thinly as possible. Dry the slices well with paper towels, as any remaining moisture will prevent the vegetables from browning quickly.

Heat 2 inches of oil in a deep saucepan (or more for a deep-fat fryer, if you have one) over medium-high heat until it reaches 350°F on a candy thermometer.

Fry the vegetable slices a few at a time so that they don't stick together. Fry until lightly colored and crisp, about 1 minute. Using a slotted spoon (or the deep-fryer basket), transfer the chips to a double layer of paper towels to drain. Season with salt to taste and serve, or cool and store in an airtight container at room temperature for up to 1 week.

*Nutritional Analysis per Serving (24 chips): calories 60, carbohydrates 7 g, fiber 2 g, protein 1 g, fat 4 g, sodium 74 mg, sugar 2 g*

# Curried Almonds

These are simple to make and offer considerably more excitement than a handful of plain, raw almonds for a snack. Chopped, they make an excellent garnish for grilled poultry or fish.

---

4 cups blanched almonds

½ cup unsalted butter

1 tablespoon hot curry powder

2 teaspoons garlic salt, or to taste

---

Preheat the oven to 300°F. Line a rimmed baking sheet with parchment paper.

Place the almonds on the prepared baking sheet in a single layer. Transfer to the preheated oven and roast until golden brown, about 25 minutes.

Place the butter in a small saucepan over medium heat. Add the curry powder and garlic salt and cook, stirring, until melted and aromatic, about 3 minutes.

Pour the butter mixture over the baked almonds, tossing to coat well, and continue to bake, stirring occasionally, until well coated and glazed, about 15 minutes more.

Remove from the oven and, using a slotted spoon, transfer the almonds to a double layer of paper towels to drain. Serve immediately, or cool and store in an airtight container at room temperature for up to 10 days.

*Nutritional Analysis per Serving (6 almonds): calories 44, carbohydrates 2 g, fiber 1 g, protein 2 g, fat 4 g, sodium 24 mg, sugar 0 g*

# French-Fried Almonds

With this recipe, you have to make sure that you fry the almonds long enough to get them crisp but not so long that they burn. This can happen very quickly, so watch carefully as you cook.

---

½ cup plus 2 tablespoons coconut oil

1 pound raw almonds

Seasoned salt

---

Heat the oil in a large frying pan over medium-high heat. When melted, lower the heat to medium and add the almonds. Fry, stirring frequently, until the almonds are brown and crispy, about 7 minutes.

Using a slotted spoon, transfer the almonds to a double layer of paper towels to drain. When drained, sprinkle with seasoned salt to taste and allow to cool. Serve immediately, or store in an airtight container at room temperature for up to 10 days.

*Nutritional Analysis per Serving (6 almonds): calories 212, carbohydrates 7 g, fiber 4 g, protein 7 g, fat 19 g, sodium 83 mg, sugar 1 g*

# Chili Nuts

MAKES 8 CUPS

If you like, you can add some pumpkin or sunflower seeds to this mix. Watch carefully as the nuts cook so that they reach the perfect degree of golden goodness without a hint of char.

---

2 cups raw cashews

2 cups raw pecans

2 cups raw walnuts

2 cups pistachios

$\frac{1}{3}$ cup unsalted butter, melted

1 tablespoon chili powder

$\frac{1}{2}$ teaspoon cayenne pepper

$\frac{1}{2}$ teaspoon garlic salt

---

Preheat the oven to 300°F. Line two large rimmed baking sheets with parchment paper.

Place the nuts on the prepared baking sheets in a single layer. Transfer to the preheated oven and roast, stirring occasionally, until golden brown, about 25 minutes.

Combine the melted butter with the chili powder, cayenne, and garlic salt and pour the mixture over the hot nuts, tossing to coat. Continue to roast, stirring frequently, until shiny, golden brown, and crisp, about 15 minutes more.

Remove from the oven and, using a slotted spoon, transfer to a double layer of paper towels to drain and cool. Serve immediately, or store in an airtight container at room temperature for up to 10 days.

*Nutritional Analysis per Serving (6 nuts): calories 190, carbohydrates 6 g, fiber 2 g, protein 5 g, fat 17 g, sodium 16 mg, sugar 2 g*

# Deviled Nuts

MAKES 1 POUND

Smoke and spice is what you get with this nut combo. These are great for snacking or for passing around with a glass of red wine at cocktail time. This recipe may also be used with pumpkin seeds.

---

3 tablespoons clarified butter (see page 42), ghee, or unsalted butter

1 pound mixed roasted unsalted nuts, such as cashews, almonds, hazelnuts, walnuts, and/or pecans

Dash Worcestershire sauce

1½ teaspoons salt

¼ teaspoon cayenne pepper

¼ teaspoon smoked paprika

¼ teaspoon ground dried chiles, such as ancho

⅛ teaspoon ground cumin

---

Heat the clarified butter in a large frying pan over medium heat. Add the nuts and fry, stirring frequently, until golden, about 5 minutes. Add a dash of Worcestershire sauce and stir to blend.

Using a slotted spoon, transfer to a double layer of paper towels to drain. When well drained, place the nuts in a resealable plastic bag along with the salt, cayenne, paprika, ground chiles, and cumin. Seal and shake vigorously to evenly coat the nuts with the spices.

Pour out onto a baking sheet and set aside to cool. Serve immediately, or store in an airtight container at room temperature for up to 10 days.

*Nutritional Analysis per Serving (6 nuts): calories 219, carbohydrates 6 g, fiber 3 g, protein 6 g, fat 20 g, sodium 251 mg, sugar 1 g*

# Spiced Cheese Pot

MAKES ABOUT 3 CUPS

Rather than just a plain hunk of cheese for a snack, try this slightly spicy mix. It is particularly good spooned onto a lettuce or endive leaf or packed into a celery stick for an afternoon pick-me-up.

---

1 pound grated sharp cheddar cheese

1/3 cup coconut oil

3 tablespoons minced shallot or onion

2 tablespoons minced fresh chives

1 tablespoon Dijon mustard

1 teaspoon hot curry powder

1/2 teaspoon cayenne pepper

---

Combine the cheese, coconut oil, shallot, chives, mustard, curry powder, and cayenne in the bowl of a food processor fitted with the metal blade. Process until smooth. Scrape from the processor bowl into a bowl and serve, or cover and store in an airtight container in the refrigerator for up to 2 weeks.

*Nutritional Analysis per Serving (2 tablespoons): calories 103, carbohydrates 1 g, fiber 0 g, protein 5 g, fat 9 g, sodium 137 mg, sugar 0 g*

# Saganaki

MAKES 1 POUND

Saganaki is a traditional Greek meze or appetizer/snack, often served after being flamed with ouzo, a Greek liqueur, on the stove or at the table. The word comes from the name of the pan, or *sagani*, in which the cheese is usually fried. The oil has to be very hot so that the cheese browns quickly before it melts completely. Saganaki is often served with tomatoes, olives, and, in Greece, lots of bread. It is normally dusted with flour, but I find that the delicate almond flavor adds a lovely accent to the slightly acidic cheese.

⅔ cup almond meal

1 pound halloumi, kefalotyri, or kasseri cheese (or Pecorino Romano or feta)

½ cup extra-virgin olive oil

1 lemon, quartered, for serving

Place the almond meal in one shallow bowl and about 2 cups of cold water in another.

Using a sharp knife, cut the cheese into sticks that are about ½ inch thick and 3 inches long. Working with one piece at a time, dip into the cold water, allowing the excess water to drip off. Then, dredge in the almond meal, again allowing the excess to fall off. Transfer the pieces to a baking sheet as they are dredged.

Heat the olive oil in a large frying pan over medium heat. Add the cheese and fry, turning once, until golden and crusty on both sides, about 2 minutes. Remove from the heat and serve immediately, with a spritz of lemon juice.

*Nutritional Analysis per Serving (1 piece): calories 245, carbohydrates 3 g, fiber 1 g, protein 14 g, fat 24 g, sodium 603 mg, sugar 0 g*

# Marinated Olives

You can make as many of these aromatic olives as you like; however, it is easiest to make and store them in 8-ounce containers. I suggest pitted olives only for their convenience; if you are partial to a particular type of olive, by all means use it.

---

8 ounces pitted mixed olives

2 garlic cloves, peeled and sliced

1 dried chile

1 small rosemary sprig

Extra-virgin olive oil

Red wine vinegar

---

Place half of the olives in a half-pint container with a tight-fitting lid. Add the garlic, chile, and rosemary and cover with the remaining olives. Fill the container two-thirds full with oil and top off with vinegar. Cover and shake vigorously to mix.

Marinate in the refrigerator for at least 2 days before serving. Leftovers can be covered and stored in the refrigerator for up to 1 month.

*Nutritional Analysis per Serving (6 olives): calories 90, carbohydrates 3 g, fiber 0 g, protein 1 g, fat 9 g, sodium 642 mg, sugar 0 g*

# Deviled Eggs

MAKES 24

If you go to the trouble of making deviled eggs, you might as well start with a dozen eggs because everyone loves them and they will disappear faster than you can imagine. If you want to get fancy, add finely minced shrimp, crabmeat, or anchovies to the yolks and garnish with a tiny parsley or cilantro leaf. Or add some chopped fresh flat-leaf parsley, mint, basil, or cilantro to the mix to vary the flavor.

---

12 large hard-boiled eggs (see page 93), peeled

¼ cup Mayonnaise (page 40)

1 tablespoon Dijon mustard, or more to taste

Pinch cayenne pepper

White vinegar, optional

Salt and pepper

Paprika, for optional garnish

---

Carefully cut the eggs in half lengthwise. Gently remove the yolks and place them in a small mixing bowl. Set the whites aside.

Add the mayonnaise, mustard, and cayenne pepper to the egg yolks. Using a kitchen fork, mash the mixture together. If the mixture seems too dry, add a bit more mayo or mustard or a couple drops of vinegar. Season with salt and pepper to taste.

Scrape the mixture into a pastry bag fitted with a small star tip and carefully pipe an equal portion of the mashed yolk mixture into each white half, mounding slightly. (Alternatively, you can simply use a teaspoon to portion the yolk mixture into the whites.) Lightly dust with paprika, if desired.

Serve immediately, or cover lightly with plastic wrap and refrigerate for up to 8 hours.

*Nutritional Analysis per Serving (2 halves): calories 167, carbohydrates 2 g, fiber 0 g, protein 10 g, fat 14 g, sodium 229 mg, sugar 1 g*

# Chicken Liver Pâté

Pâté makes a superb snacking treat, as it is filling and extremely nutritious. I like to serve it with celery, red bell pepper, cucumber sticks, or endive leaves. This one is uncomplicated to make and keeps well in an airtight container in the refrigerator for up to 1 week. If you are storing for more than a day or so, melt about ¼ cup unsalted butter and pour it over the pâté. Once the butter hardens, the top is sealed and the pâté remains fresh. You don't even have to scrape off the butter when serving; it simply becomes part of the pâté.

---

8 ounces chicken livers, well trimmed

½ cup water

½ cup chopped onion

½ teaspoon chopped garlic

1 bay leaf

¼ teaspoon chopped fresh sage

¼ teaspoon chopped fresh thyme

Salt

1 tablespoon dry sherry

¾ cup unsalted butter, at room temperature

Pepper

---

Combine the chicken livers, water, onion, garlic, bay leaf, sage, and thyme in a medium saucepan over medium-low heat. Season with salt to taste and bring to a simmer. Cover, reduce the heat to low, and cook until the livers are just barely cooked, about 5 minutes. Remove from the heat and set aside for 5 minutes.

Remove and discard the bay leaf. Pour the liver mixture into a fine-mesh strainer set over a mixing bowl and discard the liquid.

Transfer the drained liver mixture to the bowl of a food processor fitted with the metal blade. Add the sherry and process until chopped. With the motor running, begin adding the butter, a bit at a time, processing until all of the butter has been incorporated and the pâté is completely smooth. Season with salt and pepper to taste.

Scrape the mixture into a serving bowl, smoothing down the top until even. Place a piece of plastic wrap directly on the pâté and chill in the refrigerator until very firm, at least 2 hours. Serve.

*Nutritional Analysis per Serving (2 tablespoons): calories 82, carbohydrates 1 g, fiber 0 g, protein 3 g, fat 7 g, sodium 72 mg, sugar 0 g*

# Artichoke Dip

Artichoke dip came into its own in the 1960s, and there have been iterations of it for almost every generation since then. I've updated the old standby with two delicious but healthier versions here, one cold and one hot; both work equally well with raw vegetables. The cold one is fine for everyday dipping and the hot for an appetizer or hors d'oeuvre when company's coming.

### COLD

1 (15-ounce) can artichoke hearts, well drained

½ cup Mayonnaise (page 10)

1 tablespoon chopped fresh basil, flat-leaf parsley, or chives

Salt and pepper

Place the artichoke hearts in the bowl of a food processor fitted with the metal blade. Add the mayonnaise and herbs, season with salt and pepper to taste, and process until almost smooth—you want to see a little texture in the mix. Scrape from the processor into a serving bowl and serve. Leftovers can be covered and stored in the refrigerator for up to 2 days.

### HOT

1 recipe Cold Artichoke Dip

1 (10-ounce) package frozen chopped spinach or kale,
    thawed and well drained

1 teaspoon minced garlic

¾ cup grated Parmesan cheese

½ cup shredded mozzarella cheese

Salt and pepper, optional

Preheat the oven to 350°F. Generously butter the interior of a 9-inch round baking dish or pie plate and set aside.

Combine the cold dip with the spinach and garlic, stirring to blend well. Add ½ cup of the Parmesan cheese along with the mozzarella and again stir to blend well. Taste and, if necessary, add salt and pepper to taste.

Scrape the mixture into the prepared baking dish, smoothing the top with a rubber spatula. Sprinkle the remaining ¼ cup Parmesan over the top. Transfer to the preheated oven and bake until cooked through and golden brown on top, about 20 minutes. Remove from the oven and serve. Leftovers can be covered and stored in the refrigerator for up to 3 days; bring to room temperature, cover with aluminum foil, and reheat in a preheated 350°F oven for about 7 minutes.

*Cold Dip: Nutritional Analysis per Serving (2 tablespoons): calories 67, carbohydrates 5 g, fiber 1 g, protein 1 g, fat 6 g, sodium 188 mg, sugar 2 g*

*Hot Dip: Nutritional Analysis per Serving (2 tablespoons): calories 227, carbohydrates 11 g, fiber 3 g, protein 9 g, fat 16 g, sodium 610 mg, sugar 4 g*

# Celery Stuffed with Cashew Butter

MAKES 16 PIECES

This is a new take on that old childhood favorite, peanut butter–stuffed celery. These celery sticks will keep, tightly covered and refrigerated, for about 3 days. Or you can just make the cashew butter mix and keep it on hand to make a stuffed celery stick whenever the snacking mood hits. If you are feeling artistic, store the mix in a pastry bag fitted with the star tip and run a star-shaped line down the celery groove.

6 ounces cashew butter

3 ounces soft goat cheese

1 teaspoon freshly grated orange zest

Tabasco sauce

16 medium celery ribs, trimmed and chilled

¼ cup chopped toasted cashews, optional

Combine the cashew butter, goat cheese, orange zest, and Tabasco in the bowl of a food processor fitted with the metal blade. Process until well blended and very smooth.

Spread an equal portion of the cashew butter mix down the groove in each piece of celery. If desired, sprinkle chopped cashews on top, and serve.

*Nutritional Analysis per Serving (1 stick): calories 97, carbohydrates 5 g, fiber 1 g, protein 3 g, fat 7 g, sodium 54 mg, sugar 2 g*

# Endive Leaves with Caponata

MAKES 8

Since I know you always have homemade caponata on hand (right?), this could become an everyday snack. The recipe couldn't be simpler. One head of endive will yield quite a few leaves, but they will, for the most part, be of varying sizes, so a tablespoon on one huge leaf might look a bit skimpy, whereas on a small leaf it might just ooze over the top. Since you're snacking, it shouldn't matter.

8 large endive leaves

½ cup Caponata (page 125)

Trim the bottom edge from the endive leaves. Spoon 1 tablespoon caponata in the center of each and serve.

*Nutritional Analysis per Serving (1 large leaf with 1 tablespoon caponata): calories 93, carbohydrates 10 g, fiber 3 g, protein 1 g, fat 6 g, sodium 237 mg, sugar 4 g*

# Stuffed Mushrooms

MAKES 16

These are quite different from those bready baked stuffed mushrooms that were found on the banquet and party circuit for years. These mushrooms are cooked and then covered with a fresh tomato mix, almost like a salsa. You can prepare both the mushrooms and the tomatoes ahead of time and then fill the mushrooms whenever the snack urge hits you.

16 large button mushroom caps

¼ cup extra-virgin olive oil

2 cups chopped peeled and seeded tomatoes or canned diced tomatoes, drained

1 bunch scallions, trimmed and chopped

1 garlic clove, chopped

1 tablespoon chopped fresh basil

¼ cup chopped fresh chives

1 teaspoon freshly squeezed lemon juice

Salt and pepper

Parmesan, for shaving, optional

Preheat the oven to 350°F. Line a small baking sheet with parchment paper.

Lay the mushrooms on the prepared baking sheet, cap-side down. Drizzle ½ teaspoon olive oil over each mushroom. Transfer to the preheated oven and roast just until barely cooked through and coloring slightly, about 15 minutes. Remove from the oven and set aside to cool.

Combine the tomatoes, scallions, garlic, and basil in the bowl of a food processor fitted with the metal blade. Process, using quick on and off turns, for just a second or two. You want the mixture to blend, but not puree.

Scrape the mixture into a mixing bowl. Stir in the chives, lemon juice, and remaining olive oil and season with salt and pepper to taste. Let marinate for about 15 minutes to allow the flavors to marry.

When ready to serve, drain the tomato mixture well in a fine-mesh sieve. Mound an equal portion into each mushroom. If desired, shave a piece of Parmesan over the top, and serve.

*Nutritional Analysis per Serving (1 mushroom): calories 39, carbohydrates 2 g, fiber 0 g, protein 1 g, fat 4 g, sodium 39 mg, sugar 1 g*

# Marinated Almond Mushrooms

You will usually find marinated mushrooms flavored with Italian herbs and spices, but this version reminds me of the South of France, where blossoming almond trees herald the early spring. They are a light and appealing have-on-hand snack for any time of the year.

3 cups quartered button mushrooms

½ cup toasted sliced almonds

½ cup almond oil

2 tablespoons sherry wine vinegar

1 tablespoon slivered fresh mint leaves

Salt and white pepper

Combine the mushrooms and the almonds in a mixing bowl. Add the oil, vinegar, and mint, stirring to blend. Season with salt and white pepper to taste, cover, and let marinate at room temperature for 1 hour before serving. Leftovers may be covered and stored in the refrigerator for up to 1 week; bring back to room temperature before serving.

*Nutritional Analysis per Serving (2 tablespoons): calories 41, carbohydrates 1 g, fiber 0 g, protein 1 g, fat 4 g, sodium 58 mg, sugar 0 g*

# Cauliflower "Hummus"

MAKES ABOUT 4 CUPS

Here's our old friend cauliflower working its magic again. Its sweet, mellow flavor is just the right complement for the rich tahini. If you can find Meyer lemons, their juice is a bit less acidic than regular lemons and adds a hint of sweetness to the mix. Raw or cooked vegetables cut into sticks or rounds are great for dipping. This "hummus" can also be thinned with a bit of chicken stock (page 33) to make a sauce for grilled vegetables or even a chicken breast or fish fillet.

---

1 head cauliflower, trimmed and broken into small florets

2 tablespoons extra-virgin olive oil

3 garlic cloves

Juice of 1 lemon, preferably a Meyer lemon

Freshly grated zest of 1 orange

½ cup tahini

1 teaspoon ground cumin

Tabasco sauce

½ teaspoon salt

---

Preheat the oven to 450°F. Line a rimmed baking sheet with parchment paper and set aside.

Place the cauliflower in a medium mixing bowl and add the olive oil, tossing to coat well. Transfer the oiled cauliflower to the prepared baking sheet and place in the preheated oven. Roast, turning occasionally, until lightly colored and tender, about 20 minutes.

Remove from the oven and place in the bowl of a food processor fitted with the metal blade. Add the garlic, lemon juice, orange zest, tahini, cumin, and Tabasco to taste and process to a smooth, thick puree. Add the salt and process to incorporate. Scrape into a nonreactive container and serve immediately. Leftovers may be covered and stored in the refrigerator for up to 1 week; bring back to room temperature before serving.

*Nutritional Analysis per Serving (2 tablespoons): calories 37, carbohydrates 2 g, fiber 1 g, protein 1 g, fat 3 g, sodium 82 mg, sugar 0 g*

# Eggplant-Walnut Dip

MAKES ABOUT 2 CUPS

This interesting mixture works equally well as a dip with raw vegetables and as a sauce with cooked vegetables. It keeps well for a couple of weeks (covered and refrigerated), so it's an excellent make-ahead snack source.

---

1 pound eggplant, cut lengthwise into ¼-inch-thick slices

3 tablespoons walnut oil, plus more if necessary

¼ cup extra-virgin olive oil

2 cups chopped onion

1 tablespoon chopped garlic

5 ounces Pecorino Romano cheese, cut into small pieces

1¼ cups toasted walnuts

1 packed cup fresh basil leaves

1 tablespoon balsamic vinegar

Salt and pepper

---

Preheat and oil the grill or preheat the broiler.

Generously brush both sides of the eggplant slices with walnut oil. Place in a single layer on the grill and grill, turning occasionally, until cooked through and nicely browned, about 10 minutes. Remove from the grill and set aside to cool.

Alternatively, place a single layer of oiled eggplant slices on an oiled broiler pan under the hot broiler, about 3 inches from the flame. Broil until golden brown, about 4 minutes. Turn and broil the other side until golden, about 4 minutes more. If the eggplant seems dry, brush with additional walnut oil as it cooks. Remove from the broiler and allow to cool. This may have to be done in batches, depending on the size of your broiler.

Heat the olive oil in a large frying pan over medium heat. Add the onion and garlic and cook, stirring frequently, until golden brown, about 12 minutes.

Scrape the onion mixture into the bowl of a food processor fitted with the metal blade. Add the cooled eggplant, along with the cheese, walnuts, basil, and vinegar. Season with salt and pepper to taste and process until almost smooth. Do not puree. Scrape the mixture into a serving bowl and serve.

*Nutritional Analysis per Serving (2 tablespoons): calories 176, carbohydrates 6 g, fiber 2 g, protein 7 g, fat 15 g, sodium 180 mg, sugar 2 g*

# DESSERTS

---

ENJOYING A LITTLE SWEETNESS after a hearty meal is very much a part of our culture. Just because you're significantly reducing your sugar intake doesn't mean you can't find a satisfying dessert using ingredients like dark chocolate, coconut, and nut butters. Here are just a few ideas to satisfy that sweet tooth. Of course, the simplest thing to do is to break off a piece of rich, dark (over 70 percent cacao) chocolate and nibble away, but once in a while you might want a bit more to chew on in this department. I think you will find that all of these desserts are up to the challenge. Just remember: indulgence is just that—it is not something that should be in your daily routine.

# Coconut Bursts

This recipe couldn't be easier or a more perfect *Grain Brain* dessert. It also works as a super late-afternoon pick-me-up. You can use any toasted nut in place of the coconut or combine nuts with the coconut if you like.

---

8 ounces bittersweet (at least 70% cacao) chocolate, chopped

1 cup toasted unsweetened coconut flakes

---

Line a baking sheet with waxed paper and set aside.

Bring a few inches of water to a boil in the bottom half of a double boiler set over high heat. Place the chocolate in the top half of the double boiler and set it on the bottom half. Heat, stirring frequently, until the chocolate is almost melted, about 5 minutes. Remove from the heat and whisk until completely melted. Add the coconut and stir to combine.

Drop the mixture by the spoonful onto the prepared baking sheet. Set aside to cool and firm up. Serve, or store in an airtight container in layers separated by waxed paper for up to 2 weeks.

*Nutritional Analysis per Serving (1 piece): calories 50, carbohydrates 4 g, fiber 1 g, protein 1 g, fat 4 g, sodium 1 mg, sugar 2 g*

# Chocolate-Dipped Almonds

MAKES 1 POUND

Here is another simple, delightful treat. Just remember to buy high-quality chocolate—it will take these nuts from ordinary to extraordinary. If you think you are going to make these often, it helps to have an inexpensive chocolate dipping fork on hand. They are available at confectionary supply stores or online.

---

1 pound raw almonds

8 ounces bittersweet (at least 70% cacao) chocolate, chopped

---

Preheat the oven to 300°F. Line a baking sheet with waxed paper and set aside.

Line a rimmed baking sheet with parchment paper. Spread the almonds out in a single layer on the baking sheet. Transfer to the preheated oven and toast until golden brown and aromatic, about 15 minutes. Remove from the oven and set aside to cool.

Bring a few inches of water to a boil in the bottom half of a double boiler set over high heat. Place the chocolate in the top half of the double boiler and set it on the bottom half. Heat, stirring frequently, until the chocolate is almost melted, about 5 minutes. Remove from the heat and whisk until completely melted.

Working with one almond at a time, dip either one end or the whole almond into the chocolate, allowing the excess to drip off. If you are dipping just one end, hold the nut in your fingertips; if you want to dip the whole nut, lay it on a kitchen fork and dip it into the chocolate.

Place the chocolate-coated nut on the waxed paper–lined baking sheet and set aside to harden. Serve, or store in an airtight container in layers separated by waxed paper for up to 2 weeks.

*Nutritional Analysis per Serving (3 almonds): calories 28, carbohydrates 2 g, fiber 1 g, protein 1 g, fat 2 g, sodium 0 mg, sugar 1 g*

# Coconut-Cashew Bars

MAKES ABOUT 16

Somewhere between a candy and a cookie, these rich bars are an unexpected and satisfying treat. You can change the flavor by varying the nut butter and the nut garnish.

---

1 cup shredded unsweetened coconut

½ cup cashew butter

2 tablespoons almond meal

2 tablespoons coconut oil, melted

1 tablespoon stevia powder

1 teaspoon pure vanilla extract

4 ounces bittersweet (at least 70% cacao) chocolate, chopped

½ cup toasted cashew pieces

---

Preheat the oven to 325°F. Line the bottom of an 8-inch square baking pan with parchment paper and set aside.

Combine the coconut, cashew butter, almond meal, coconut oil, stevia, and vanilla in the bowl of a standing electric mixer fitted with the paddle. Beat on low until the mixture has blended completely, about 4 minutes.

Using a rubber spatula, spread the coconut mixture into the prepared baking pan, smoothing the top evenly. Transfer to the preheated oven and bake just until the edges begin to pull away from the pan and color slightly, about 12 minutes. Remove the pan from the oven and place it on a wire rack to cool.

Bring a few inches of water to a boil in the bottom half of a double boiler set over high heat. Place the chocolate in the top half of the double boiler and set it on the bottom half. Heat, stirring frequently, until the chocolate is almost melted, about 5 minutes. Remove from the heat and whisk until completely melted.

Pour the melted chocolate over the cooled coconut mixture, smoothing the top with an offset spatula or rubber spatula. Sprinkle the cashew pieces evenly over the top and set aside to harden.

Using a serrated knife, cut into 16 bars. Serve, or store in an airtight container in layers separated by waxed paper for up to 1 week.

*Nutritional Analysis per Serving (1 bar): calories 169, carbohydrates 9 g, fiber 2 g, protein 3 g, fat 14 g, sodium 3 mg, sugar 3 g*

# Chocolate-Hazelnut Truffles

These truffles are beautiful to look at and make for a very special treat. Although I use hazelnuts here, don't hesitate to use other nuts or even a variety of nuts. If you do use other nuts (macadamia nuts would make an interesting choice), replace the hazelnut extract with pure vanilla extract.

---

8 ounces bittersweet (at least 70% cacao) chocolate, finely chopped

½ cup heavy cream

1 teaspoon pure hazelnut extract

½ cup sifted unsweetened dark cocoa powder

About 50 toasted hazelnuts

---

Place the chocolate in a heatproof bowl set over a saucepan of very hot water.

Place the cream in a small saucepan over low heat and cook just until bubbles appear around the edge of the pan. Remove from the heat and pour the hot cream over the melting chocolate. Let it sit for about 30 seconds. Add the extract and, using a wooden spoon, beat the cream into the chocolate. When completely blended, set aside to cool. When cool, cover and refrigerate until well chilled, about 2 hours.

Line a rimmed baking sheet with waxed paper and set aside.

Place the cocoa powder in a large shallow bowl or plate and set aside.

Using a small melon-baller or your hands, scoop up a small amount (about 1 teaspoon) of the chilled chocolate. Push a toasted hazelnut into the chocolate ganache and then re-form the chocolate into a small, evenly shaped ball surrounding the nut. Drop the ball into the cocoa powder and lightly toss to coat. Transfer to the waxed paper–lined baking sheet and continue making truffles.

Serve immediately, or store in an airtight container in layers separated by waxed paper in the refrigerator for up to 1 week. Bring back to room temperature before serving.

**NOTE:** Instead of cocoa powder, you can roll the truffles in about 1 cup very finely chopped hazelnuts, but this will change the nutritional analysis substantially.

*Nutritional Analysis per Serving (1 truffle): calories 44, carbohydrates 3 g, fiber 1 g, protein 1 g, fat 4 g, sodium 1 mg, sugar 2 g*

# Chocolate Almond Cake

SERVES 12

This is far from an everyday treat, but it is an excellent cake to make when entertaining. A small scoop of mascarpone cheese on each wedge is "the icing on the cake."

---

½ cup unsalted butter, at room temperature, plus more for buttering the pan

6 ounces bittersweet (at least 70% cacao) chocolate, chopped

1¼ cups blanched raw almonds

8 tablespoons stevia powder

3 tablespoons almond meal

2 teaspoons pure vanilla extract

6 large eggs, at room temperature

½ cup chopped almonds

---

Preheat the oven to 350°F. Lightly butter the bottom and sides of a 9-inch springform pan and then line it with parchment paper. Set aside.

Bring a few inches of water to a boil in the bottom half of a double boiler set over high heat. Combine the chocolate and butter in the top half of the double boiler and set it on the bottom half. Heat, stirring frequently, until melted and completely blended, about 5 minutes. Remove from the heat and set aside.

Place the almonds and 2 tablespoons of the stevia in the bowl of a food processor fitted with the metal blade and process until it resembles coarse sand. Do not overprocess or the nuts will turn to butter. Scrape the almond mixture into the chocolate and add the almond meal, stirring to blend well.

Place the eggs in the bowl of a standing electric mixer fitted with the balloon whip. Add the remaining 6 tablespoons stevia and beat on high until light yellow and tripled in volume, about 7 minutes.

Remove the bowl from the mixer and carefully fold the chocolate mixture into the eggs until there is no evidence of egg.

Pour the batter into the prepared pan and place in the preheated oven. Bake for 15 minutes; then, sprinkle the chopped almonds over the top. Continue to bake until the cake is set in the center, about 15 minutes more.

Remove the pan from the oven and place it on a wire rack to cool for 45 minutes. Then, run a knife around the edge to ensure that the cake will easily come away from the sides. Remove the outside ring. Transfer the cake to a cake plate and set aside to cool completely before cutting into small wedges and serving.

*Nutritional Analysis per Serving (1 slice): calories 310, carbohydrates 13 g, fiber 4 g, protein 9 g, fat 27 g, sodium 36 mg, sugar 6 g*

# Chocolate Avocado Pudding

SERVES 4

Don't be skeptical...this really does make a tasty pudding. You need soft, ripe avocados with no brown spots and excellent dark (at least 70 percent cacao) cocoa powder to achieve phenomenal texture and flavor.

---

2 avocados, peeled, pitted, and cut into pieces

½ cup unsweetened almond milk

⅓ cup unsweetened dark cocoa powder

3 tablespoons liquid stevia

2 tablespoons almond butter

1 teaspoon pure vanilla extract

16 raspberries, for optional garnish

---

Combine the avocados, almond milk, cocoa powder, stevia, almond butter, and vanilla in the bowl of a food processor fitted with the metal blade. Process until smooth. Spoon the "pudding" into four small bowls and serve, garnished with a few raspberries, if desired.

*Nutritional Analysis per Serving: calories 245, carbohydrates 14 g, fiber 9 g, protein 5 g, fat 21 g, sodium 48 mg, sugar 2 g*

# Lemon Soufflé Pudding

SERVES 6

This light dessert looks spectacular. Serve it warm, or cover and refrigerate it for up to 8 hours for a refreshing chilled treat. Rather than used simply as topping, the berries can also be folded into the pudding.

---

3 large eggs, separated

⅓ cup stevia powder

3 tablespoons tapioca starch

Pinch salt

1¾ cups cold water

Juice of 2 lemons, preferably Meyer lemons

Freshly grated zest of 1 lemon

¼ cup unsalted butter, cut into small pieces

1 teaspoon pure vanilla extract

1 cup berries of your choice, optional

---

Place the egg yolks in a small mixing bowl and beat to loosen. Set aside.

Place the egg whites in a large mixing bowl and use a hand-held electric mixer to beat until stiff peaks form. Set aside.

Combine the stevia, tapioca starch, and salt in a small saucepan. Add the cold water and whisk to blend completely. Place over medium heat and cook, stirring constantly, until thickened. Stir in the lemon juice and zest.

Stir about ¼ cup of the lemon mixture into the egg yolks to temper. Then, stir the warm egg yolk mixture into the lemon mixture. Add the butter and vanilla and continue to cook, stirring constantly, until blended and thick.

Remove from the heat and fold the hot lemon pudding into the egg whites. Continue to fold until the egg whites are completely blended and the pudding is light and fluffy. Spoon into six individual serving dishes, top with a few berries, if desired, and serve.

*Nutritional Analysis per Serving: calories 133, carbohydrates 9 g, fiber 1 g, protein 3 g, fat 10 g, sodium 33 mg, sugar 4 g*

# Baked Custard

This is about as close to an old-fashioned diner custard as you can get without using lots of cream and sugar. Although it can be served warm, the flavors will be more pronounced if the custard is allowed to cool or, even better, refrigerated until chilled. The vanilla seeds add a depth of sweetness that vanilla extract alone will not give to the finished dish.

---

2½ cups unsweetened almond milk

½ cup heavy cream

4 large eggs

2 large egg yolks

Seeds from ½ vanilla bean

⅓ cup stevia powder

2 teaspoons pure vanilla extract

Pinch salt

---

Preheat the oven to 350°F. Generously butter six 4-ounce custard dishes or one 1½-quart baking dish. Set aside.

Combine the almond milk and heavy cream in a small saucepan over medium-low heat and cook until very hot but not yet simmering, about 4 minutes. Remove from the heat.

Combine the whole eggs and egg yolks with the vanilla seeds, stevia, vanilla extract, and salt, stirring to blend. Don't whip or the eggs will get foamy and the bubbles will remain on the top of the baked custard. Strain the eggs through a medium-mesh sieve into a clean container. (This step is not essential, but it does strain out the bits of coagulated egg white.)

Stirring constantly, add about ¼ cup of the hot milk to the eggs to temper. Then, slowly stir in the remaining milk.

Place the buttered dish(es) in a large baking pan. Add cold water to come about halfway up the sides of the dish(es). (The water bath is extremely important as it keeps the outside of the custard from cooking too fast and leaving the center underdone.) Transfer to the preheated oven and bake until almost set in the center, about 25 minutes for separate custard dishes or 35 minutes for one large baking dish. It should still sway when the dishes are moved. To test, poke a small knife into the center; if it comes out clean, the custard is ready to be removed from the oven.

Remove from the oven and carefully transfer the dishes to a wire rack to finish cooking and cool slightly before serving.

*Nutritional Analysis per Serving: calories 155, carbohydrates 4 g, fiber 1 g, protein 6 g, fat 13 g, sodium 225 mg, sugar 1 g*

# Floating Island

Floating island is a classic French dessert (known as *oeufs à la neige*) that is rarely made anymore. It is uncomplicated to make and yet looks difficult when it all comes together. This version is not as sweet as the classic and is fragrant with almond rather than the usual vanilla. It is best served on the same day it is made.

---

3 extra-large eggs, at room temperature

4 tablespoons stevia powder

2 cups unsweetened almond milk

1 teaspoon pure almond extract

½ cup assorted berries, optional

2 tablespoons toasted almond slivers, optional

---

Separate 2 of the eggs. Place the 2 egg whites in the bowl of a standing electric mixer fitted with the balloon whisk and beat on medium until soft peaks form, about 3 minutes. Slowly add 2 tablespoons of the stevia and continue to beat until the whites are stiff but not dry.

Heat the almond milk in a large frying pan over medium heat. Cook until bubbles form around the edge of the pan, about 4 minutes. Using a large spoon, scoop up a large, rounded mound of egg white (about one-quarter of the total amount) and drop it into the hot milk. Continue to make 3 more floating meringues.

Bring the milk to a very gentle simmer and cook the meringues just until cooked through and a bit firm, about 5 minutes.

Using a slotted spoon, transfer the meringues from the milk to a plate, allowing the excess liquid to drop off. (Do not discard the milk.) If the meringues are still wet, pat the bottoms with a paper towel. Place the meringues in the refrigerator while you make the sauce.

Pour the hot poaching milk into a medium saucepan set over medium-low heat. Combine the 2 egg yolks with the remaining whole egg and the remaining 2 tablespoons stevia in a small mixing bowl, whisking to blend thoroughly. Add a bit of the hot milk to the egg mixture to temper; when blended, whisk the eggs into the hot milk. Cook, stirring constantly, until the custard coats the back of a spoon, about 10 minutes. Stir in the almond extract and remove from the heat.

Place the saucepan in a bowl of ice water and stir frequently to chill. Pour the custard into a shallow serving bowl, press a sheet of waxed paper over the top to keep a film from forming, and refrigerate until very cold, at least 30 minutes.

When ready to serve, remove the waxed paper and float the chilled meringues in the custard. Sprinkle a few berries and almonds over the custard, if desired, and serve.

*Nutritional Analysis per Serving: calories 105, carbohydrates 6 g, fiber 1 g, protein 6 g, fat 7 g, sodium 139 mg, sugar 3 g*

# Raw Chia Seed Pudding

SERVES 4

This easy-to-make pudding can also be made with coconut milk, which is a bit richer in flavor than almond milk. You can also add 2 tablespoons dark cocoa powder and a pinch of cinnamon for chocolate pudding. Chia seed pudding does, however, need to rest for several hours; if the chia seeds have not soaked long enough, they will cause a bit of stomach upset.

---

2 cups unsweetened almond milk

1 tablespoon almond butter

1 tablespoon stevia powder

1 teaspoon pure almond or pure vanilla extract

½ cup chia seeds

½ cup blueberries, optional

---

Combine the almond milk, almond butter, stevia, and almond extract in a blender jar and process until smooth. Add the chia seeds and process to just blend. (The whirl in the blender helps keep the seeds from clumping together.)

Pour the pudding into one large or four small serving bowls. Cover and refrigerate for 30 minutes; then, stir to make sure the seeds are evenly distributed. Cover and refrigerate for at least 8 hours or up to 2 days. Serve chilled, with a few berries on top, if desired.

*Nutritional Analysis per Serving: calories 160, carbohydrates 14 g, fiber 9 g, protein 5 g, fat 10 g, sodium 103 mg, sugar 2 g*

# Almond Meal Crêpes with Roasted Squash

SERVES 8

This dessert has its origins in the classic French crêpes suzette, but here the crêpes reflect the *Grain Brain* diet. Roasted squash may seem like an odd dessert choice, but most winter squash are inherently sweet and, when roasted, the caramelization makes them even more so.

The crêpes are quite fragile, so you should transfer them from the pan straight to the serving dish or plate. For an elegant end-of-the-meal treat, top them with a dollop of mascarpone and a few berries and/or a drizzle of melted dark chocolate. However, they are also quite tasty plain.

---

2 cups cubed (about ½ inch) winter squash, such as butternut

2 teaspoons coconut oil, plus more for cooking

1 cup almond meal

2 large eggs

¼ cup unsweetened almond milk

2 tablespoons unsalted butter, melted

1 teaspoon stevia powder

1 teaspoon pure vanilla extract

¼ cup seltzer

¼ cup chopped toasted almonds, optional

---

Preheat the oven to 375°F.

Toss the squash with the coconut oil and place on a rimmed baking sheet. Transfer to the preheated oven and roast, tossing occasionally, until golden brown and cooked through, about 15 minutes. Remove from the oven and cover loosely with a sheet of aluminum foil to keep warm while you make the crêpes. (You can also roast the squash ahead of time and reheat when ready to serve.)

Place the almond meal in a medium mixing bowl.

In a separate bowl, whisk together the eggs, almond milk, butter, stevia, and vanilla. Add the almond milk mixture to the almond meal, beating to combine. When blended, stir in the seltzer.

Lightly coat a nonstick crêpe pan or a small nonstick skillet with coconut oil and place over medium-low heat.

Using a ladle, transfer about ¼ cup of the batter to the hot pan, carefully spreading it out to form a thin pancake. Cook until firm and golden brown on the bottom, about 90 seconds. Carefully flip the crêpe and cook until set and golden brown, another minute or so. If desired, you can stack the finished crêpes on a warm plate, separating them with sheets of waxed paper to keep them from sticking together.

Continue making crêpes until all of the batter has been used; you should have enough batter for 8 crêpes. Serve with a spoonful of roasted squash in the center of each crêpe and, if desired, a sprinkle of toasted almonds.

*Nutritional Analysis per Serving (1 crêpe): calories 113, carbohydrates 5 g, fiber 2 g, protein 3 g, fat 10 g, sodium 23 mg, sugar 1 g*

# Coconut-Lime Granita

SERVES 6

Granita is certainly not ice cream, but it is a refreshing treat nonetheless. It is nice to have on hand for a last-minute dessert.

---

1½ cups coconut milk

2 tablespoons freshly squeezed lime juice

2 tablespoons liquid stevia

1 cup cold water

---

Combine the coconut milk, lime juice, and stevia in a medium bowl. When blended, stir in the cold water. Pour into a shallow container and place in the freezer until completely frozen, about 3 hours

Using a kitchen fork, scrape back and forth over the top to shave the granita into flakes. Serve immediately. Any remaining granita will keep, frozen, for up to 2 weeks.

*Nutritional Analysis per Serving: calories 53, carbohydrates 2 g, fiber 0 g, protein 0 g,*
*fat 5 g, sodium 7 mg, sugar 0 g*

# ACKNOWLEDGMENTS

---

Just as I was beginning to celebrate the success of *Grain Brain*, the demand for a cookbook plunged me quickly back into writing mode with another cadre of creative, indefatigable individuals who helped me put this together. And once again I found myself at the mercy of experts in the publishing sphere (especially those with more experience than I in the kitchen to craft recipes worthy of publication) who made it all happen seamlessly—and deliciously.

First, I must collectively thank all the scientists and fellow colleagues who've gone before me in exploring the health and functionality of the human brain and whose research has informed the lessons and dietary recommendations I write about today. Thanks also to my patients, who are often my greatest sources of new knowledge.

Thank you to Bonnie Solow, my friend and literary agent who has been with me since day one in helping me promulgate my message about the true path to optimal brain health. You've been a steadfast champion in my mission to end brain disease and I am forever grateful for the opportunities you've provided. If it weren't for your insights, patience, gracious leadership, and attention to details, we might never have gotten the chance to pen this important culinary guide.

To Judie Choate, my kitchen comrade in creating an exquisite menu of options. Indeed, as a notable chef, writer, and "pioneer in the promotion of American food," you were essential in the process of meeting my guidelines while never losing an ounce of flavor. And to your husband, Steve Pool, who brought these meals to life with his beautiful photography.

To Kristin Loberg, my *Grain Brain* collaborator, who helped to ensure the continuity of my writing as we shifted to this cookbook. As before, while the content of my information represents my research and professional experience, it is wholly through your wordsmithing that I can convey my message to a broad readership.

To the tireless team at Little, Brown that has been a partner with me in so many ways. I bow down to Michael Pietsch, Reagan Arthur, Heather Fain, Miriam Parker, Nicole Dewey, Cathy Gruhn, Tracy Williams, Andy LeCount, Jean Garnett, and especially my editor, Tracy Behar, who combed through every sentence with her knack for keeping everything succinct and clear. It has been and remains a pleasure to work with such a dedicated, professional group.

To James Murphy, Andrew Luer, and John D'Orazio of Proton Enterprises for your incredible skill in seeing the big picture from a management perspective.

To Digital Natives, my savvy tech team responsible for making my website come alive as a companion to my books.

To my wife, Leize. Thank you for all the time and commitment in lovingly preparing the recipes. I am grateful beyond measure to have you in my life.

# INDEX

chicken *(cont.)*
    Pesto-Roasted Chicken, 212–14
    Sesame Chicken, 230
    Spicy Chicken Burgers with Guacamole, 116–17
chicken stock, Basic Stock, 33–34
Child, Julia, 42
Chiles Stuffed with Goat Cheese, 263–64
Chili Nuts, 279
Chilled Avocado Soup, 79
Chimichurri, 44
chocolate
    Chocolate Almond Cake, 307–8
    Chocolate Avocado Pudding, 309
    Chocolate-Dipped Almonds, 302
    Chocolate-Hazelnut Truffles, 305–6
cholesterol
    brain health and, 12–14
    dietary fat and, 11
    eggs and, 12, 13–14
chronic conditions, role of inflammation in, 7, 14
cilantro
    Chicken Curry with Cilantro Chutney, 225–27
    Cilantro Chutney, 225, 226–27
Cioppino, 257–58
clarified butter, 42–43
coconut
    Broccoli in Coconut Sauce, 133
    Coconut Bursts, 301
    Coconut-Cashew Bars, 303–4
    Coconut-Chicken Soup, 80–81
    Coconut-Lime Granita, 319
    Grilled Coconut-Sesame Chicken with Jicama-Cucumber Relish, 215–16
    Mint-Coconut Salmon, 243–44
coconut flour, 19
coconut oil, 12, 22
cognitive function, 4, 8–9. *See also* brain health
Compound Butter, 168, 169
condiments, 26
costs of food, 21–22
cravings, 18
C-reactive protein, 11
Creole Crunch, 47
Creole seasoning, 255
Crunchy Pumpkin Seed Toss, 272–73

cucumbers
    Grilled Coconut-Sesame Chicken with Jicama-Cucumber Relish, 215–16
    Jicama-Cucumber Relish, 215, 216, 249
Curried Almonds, 277
Curried Pork Stew, 84–85

dairy products. *See also* cheese; eggs
    dietary fats and, 14
    foods to consume liberally, 25
    foods to consume in moderation, 29
degenerative conditions, role of inflammation in, 6–7
dementia, 4, 5, 8–9, 11–13, 15
depression
    cholesterol levels and, 13
    gluten and, 15
    role of nutrition in, 4, 5, 6, 15
desserts
    Almond Meal Crêpes with Roasted Squash, 317–18
    Baked Custard, 312–13
    Chocolate Almond Cake, 307–8
    Chocolate Avocado Pudding, 309
    Chocolate-Dipped Almonds, 302
    Chocolate-Hazelnut Truffles, 305–6
    Coconut Bursts, 301
    Coconut-Cashew Bars, 303–4
    Coconut-Lime Granita, 319
    Floating Island, 314–15
    general guidelines for, 299
    Lemon Soufflé Pudding, 310–11
    Raw Chia Seed Pudding, 316
Deviled Eggs, 284
Deviled Nuts, 280
diabetes
    dietary choices and, 17
    risks for, 14
    risks for Alzheimer's disease and, 7–8
    risks for dementia and, 9
dietary choices. *See also Grain Brain* Pantry; nutrition
    brain health and, 4, 17–19
    *Grain Brain* dietary guidelines, 17–19, 21
    high-fat, low-carb diet, 4, 6–7, 10–14, 15, 17–19
    inflammation and, 6, 7, 16–17
    low-fat, high-carb diet, 4, 6–7, 10–14
    Mediterranean diet, 11

Salmon-Avocado Salad, 105–6
Salmon Burgers with Herbed Tartar Sauce, 240–41
Salmon in Chile Broth, 238–39
Salmon Roasted in Butter and Almonds, 10, 237
Slow-Roasted Salmon with Mustard Glaze, 242
Whole Roasted Red Snapper, 247–48
wild-caught fish, 12, 22, 27
flavorings, 30
Floating Island, 314–15
food allergies, 7, 14
food labels, 15, 24
food manufacturing, 11
food recommendations. *See also* dietary choices; nutrition
  foods to avoid, 23–24
  foods to consume liberally, 24–28
  foods to eat in moderation, 28–30
free radicals, 13
free-range eggs, 22
free-range poultry, 28
French-Fried Almonds, 278
Fried Green Plantains (*Tostones*), 150, 205
fruits. *See also* lemons; limes; mangos
  dried fruits, 23
  foods to consume in moderation, 29–30
  foods to consume liberally, 25, 27
  as source of carbohydrates, 9
  for sweetener, 19

garlic
  Chicken with Forty Cloves of Garlic, 217–18
  Garlic-Herb Mussels, 121
  garlic puree, 64, 189
  Garlic Shrimp, 254
  Roasted Broccoli with Garlic, 131
genetics
  dietary choices and, 7, 16–17
  genetically engineered animal feed, 12, 22
  gluten and, 16–17
ghee, 43
ginger
  Ginger-Glazed Mahimahi, 249
  Roasted Leg of Lamb with Ginger Sauce, 187–88
glucose. *See* blood sugar
gluten

food labeling and, 15, 24
foods to avoid and, 24
*Grain Brain* dietary guidelines, 17–19
*Grain Brain* Pantry and, 21
inflammation and, 6, 14–17, 18
nongluten grains, 28–29
screening for sensitivity to, 15, 17
goat cheese
  Chicken Breasts Stuffed with Swiss Chard and Goat Cheese, 219–20
  Chiles Stuffed with Goat Cheese, 263–64
*Grain Brain* (Perlmutter)
  on brain health, 4, 5, 6
  on cholesterol, 13
  dietary guidelines, 17–19, 21
  on fats, 10
  on gluten, 14, 15
  on inflammation, 7
*Grain Brain* Pantry
  foods to avoid, 23–24
  foods to consume in moderation, 28–30
  foods to consume liberally, 24–28
  shopping guidelines, 21–22
grain-fed beef, 12
grass-fed beef, 12, 14, 22, 28
Greek Salad, 10, 91
Green Beans with Walnuts, 162, 242
Green Mango, Watercress, and Arugula Salad, 86
greens. *See also specific greens*
  Sautéed Greens, 135–36, 144
Grilled Asparagus and Spring Onions, 143
Grilled Brook Trout with Brown Butter, 246
Grilled Butterflied Leg of Lamb with Eggplant Compote, 189–91
Grilled Coconut-Sesame Chicken with Jicama-Cucumber Relish, 215–16
Grilled Parmesan Tomatoes, 148
Grilled Pork Chops with Salsa Verde, 202–3
Grilled Radicchio, 139
Grilled Spiced Flank Steak, 172
Grilled Sweet and Sour Beets, 144
Grilled Veal Chops with Arugula, 182
grocery shopping, 21–22
Gruyère cheese
  Cheese Soufflé, 112
  Gruyère-Glazed Pork Chops, 204
  Wild Mushroom Gratin, 110–11
Guacamole, 117

halibut, Herb-Grilled Halibut Steaks, 245
hazelnuts
    Chocolate-Hazelnut Truffles, 305–6
    Mushroom-Hazelnut Soup, 75–76
HDL cholesterol, 11
headaches, 4, 7, 15
health claims, 15, 24
Healthy Green Slaw, 130, 132, 245
heart disease, 4, 6, 7, 11, 13–14, 17
hemoglobin A1C, 13
herbs
    foods to consume, 22, 26
    Garlic-Herb Mussels, 121
    Herbed Tartar Sauce, 240, 241
    Herb-Grilled Halibut Steaks, 245
    Herb-Roasted Turkey Breast, 231
    Salmon Burgers with Herbed Tartar Sauce,
        240–41
    Sautéed Cherry Tomatoes in Herbs, 149, 245
high blood pressure, 8
high-carb, low-fat diet, 4, 6–7, 10–14
high-fat, low-carb diet, 4, 6–7, 10–14, 15, 17–19
Hippocrates, 4
Homemade Turkey Sausage, 56–57
hormones, 12, 22
hunger, food shopping and, 21

illness
    risk for, 3
    as trigger for inflammation, 14
immune system, 14
individually quick frozen (IQF) foods, 24–25
inflammation
    brain health and disease and, 6–7, 14, 15–17
    gluten and, 6, 14–17, 18
    high-carb diet and, 6
    high-fat, low-carb diet and, 11
    omega-3 fats and, 12
    omega-6 fats and, 12
injury, as trigger for inflammation, 14
insomnia, 4
Italian Vinaigrette, 37, 91

Jerk Chicken, 221–22
jicama
    Grilled Coconut-Sesame Chicken with
        Jicama-Cucumber Relish, 215–16
    Jicama-Cucumber Relish, 215, 216, 249
Journal of Alzheimer's Disease, 11

kale
    Kale and Bacon Frittata, 107
    Kale Chips, 274
Kennedy, John F., 6
Kohlrabi Gratin, 156–57

lamb
    Braised Lamb Shanks with Green Olives,
        194–95
    Grilled Butterflied Leg of Lamb with
        Eggplant Compote, 189–91
    Lamb and Fennel with Mint Salad, 192–93
    Quick "Moussaka," 196–97
    Roasted Leg of Lamb with Ginger Sauce,
        187–88
    Traditional Chophouse Mixed Grill,
        178–79
legumes, 29
lemons
    Cauliflower with Lemon-Parsley Butter, 158
    Chicken with Lemon and Olives, 228–29
    Lemon Soufflé Pudding, 310–11
lettuce, Thai Pork Lettuce Cups, 96–97
limes, Coconut-Lime Granita, 319
London Broil with Grilled Mushrooms,
    170–71
low-carb, high-fat diet, 4, 6–7, 10–14, 15, 17–19
low-fat, high-carb diet, 4, 6–7, 10–14
lunches
    Almond-Crusted Chicken Strips, 118–19
    Avocado-Walnut Salad, 87
    Beef and Watercress Salad, 95
    Best Beef 'n Cheese Burgers, The, 120
    Caesar Salad with Asiago Tuiles, 88–89
    Cheese Soufflé, 112
    Chef's Salad Bowl, 92–93
    Chilled Avocado Soup, 79
    Coconut-Chicken Soup, 80–81
    Curried Pork Stew, 84–85
    Falafel with Tahini Sauce, 113–15
    Garlic-Herb Mussels, 121
    general guidelines for, 71
    Greek Salad, 91
    Green Mango, Watercress, and Arugula
        Salad, 86
    Kale and Bacon Frittata, 107
    Mushroom-Hazelnut Soup, 75–76
    Niçoise Salad, 103–4
    Really Great Tomato Soup, 73–74

Salmon-Avocado Salad, 105–6

Shakshuka (Eggs in Purgatory), 108–9

Shrimp and Celery Salad, 102

Spicy Chicken Burgers with Guacamole, 116–17

Texas-Style Chili, 82–83

Thai Pork Lettuce Cups, 96–97

Tomatoes Stuffed with Shrimp Salad, 100–101

Tomatoes with Mozzarella, Avocado, and Basil, 90

Tuscan Salad, 94

Warm Rainbow Chard, Pancetta, and Almond Salad, 98–99

Wild Mushroom Gratin, 110–11

Winter Squash Soup, 77–78

mahimahi, Ginger-Glazed Mahimahi, 249

Manchego cheese, Manchego Tortilla, 67–68

mangos, Green Mango, Watercress, and Arugula Salad, 86

Marinated Almond Mushrooms, 293

Marinated Olives, 283

Mayonnaise, 40–41

meat dinners. *See also* beef; chicken; lamb; pork; turkey; veal

Adobo Pork, 205

Braised Beef Brisket, 175

Braised Lamb Shanks with Green Olives, 194–95

Calf's Liver and Onions, 185–86

Filet Mignon with Compound Butter, 168–69

Grilled Butterflied Leg of Lamb with Eggplant Compote, 189–91

Grilled Pork Chops with Salsa Verde, 202–3

Grilled Spiced Flank Steak, 172

Grilled Veal Chops with Arugula, 182

Gruyère-Glazed Pork Chops, 204

Lamb and Fennel with Mint Salad, 192–93

London Broil with Grilled Mushrooms, 170–71

Meatloaf Stuffed with Hard-Boiled Eggs, 176–77

Pork Tenderloin with Sweet Spiced Onion Jam, 200–201

Quick "Moussaka," 196–97

Roasted Leg of Lamb with Ginger Sauce, 187–88

Roast Tenderloin of Beef Wrapped in Bacon, 165

Slow-Roasted Spareribs, 207

Southwest-Style Rib-Eye Steaks, 173–74

Steak Diane, 166–67

Stir-Fried Pork with Watercress, 206

Stuffed Pork Loin, 198–99

Tex-Mex Cowboy Burgers with Tomato-Onion Salsa, 181–82

Traditional Chophouse Mixed Grill, 178–79

Veal Saltimbocca, 183–84

meatless dinners. *See also* vegetables

Baked Eggplant, Zucchini, and Tomato, 261–62

Baked Spaghetti Squash with Tomato Sauce and Parmesan Cheese, 265–66

Chiles Stuffed with Goat Cheese, 263–64

Sautéed Summer Squash "Noodles" with Butter and Cheese, 267

Meatloaf Stuffed with Hard-Boiled Eggs, 176–77

Mediterranean diet, 11

memory. *See also* Alzheimer's disease

blood sugar and, 8

gluten and, 15

*Metabolism*, 13–14

migraine headaches, 5, 15

mint

Lamb and Fennel with Mint Salad, 192–93

Mint-Coconut Salmon, 243–44

Morning Wake-Up Call, 51

movement disorders, 4, 15

mozzarella cheese, Tomatoes with Mozzarella, Avocado, and Basil, 90

muscle disorders, 15

mushrooms

Broccoli, Mushrooms, and Feta, 10, 132

London Broil with Grilled Mushrooms, 170–71

Marinated Almond Mushrooms, 293

Mushroom-Hazelnut Soup, 75–76

Stuffed Mushrooms, 291–92

Wild Mushroom Gratin, 110–11

mussels, Garlic-Herb Mussels, 121

mustard, Slow-Roasted Salmon with Mustard Glaze, 242

neuropathy, 15

*New England Journal of Medicine*, 4, 8, 11

Niçoise Salad, 103–4

nongluten grains, 28–29

nut meals, 19

nut milks, 22, 25

nutrition. *See also* dietary choices
    Alzheimer's disease and, 4–5, 6, 7–9, 17
    attention deficit hyperactivity disorder
        (ADHD) and, 4, 5, 6, 15
    depression and, 4, 5, 6, 15
    food costs and, 21–22
    role in brain health, 4, 10–11

nuts. *See also* seeds
    Almond-Crusted Chicken Strips, 118–19
    Almond Meal Crêpes with Roasted Squash,
        317–18
    Asparagus with Walnut Aioli, 141–42
    Avocado-Walnut Salad, 87
    Butternut Squash with Spinach and
        Pistachios, 151–52
    Celery Stuffed with Cashew Butter, 289
    Chili Nuts, 279
    Chocolate Almond Cake, 307–8
    Chocolate-Dipped Almonds, 302
    Chocolate-Hazelnut Truffles, 305–6
    Coconut-Cashew Bars, 303–4
    Curried Almonds, 277
    Deviled Nuts, 280
    Eggplant-Walnut Dip, 296–97
    foods to consume and, 25
    French-Fried Almonds, 278
    Green Beans with Walnuts, 162, 242
    Marinated Almond Mushrooms, 293
    Mushroom-Hazelnut Soup, 75–76
    Salmon Roasted in Butter and Almonds,
        10, 237
    as source of healthy fats, 12
    Walnut Aioli, 142
    Warm Rainbow Chard, Pancetta, and
        Almond Salad, 98–99

obesity, 7, 14

olives
    Braised Lamb Shanks with Green Olives,
        194–95
    Chicken with Lemon and Olives, 228–29
    Marinated Olives, 283

omega-3 fats, 12, 120, 252

omega-6 fats, 12

onions
    Cabbage and Onion Braise, 140
    Calf's Liver and Onions, 185–86
    Grilled Asparagus and Spring Onions, 143
    Pork Tenderloin with Sweet Spiced Onion
        Jam, 200–201
    Roasted Onion Omelet with Sun-Dried
        Tomato and Onion Chutney, 10, 63–66
    Sun-Dried Tomato and Onion Chutney,
        63, 66
    Sweet Spiced Onion Jam, 200, 201
    Tex-Mex Cowboy Burgers with Tomato-
        Onion Salsa, 181–82
    Tomato-Onion Salsa, 181, 182

orange juice, 9–10

organic eggs, 22

organ meats, 28

osteoporosis, 4

packaged/processed foods, 21, 23–24, 26

pancetta
    Brussels Sprouts with Pancetta and Sage,
        134
    Warm Rainbow Chard, Pancetta, and
        Almond Salad, 98–99

Parmesan cheese
    Baked Spaghetti Squash with Tomato
        Sauce and Parmesan Cheese, 265–66
    Grilled Parmesan Tomatoes, 148
    Sautéed Summer Squash "Noodles" with
        Butter and Cheese, 267

parsley, Cauliflower with Lemon-Parsley
        Butter, 158

Pepper Jack cheese, Turkey Cutlets with
        Roasted Peppers and Pepper Jack Cheese,
        232

peppers
    Chiles Stuffed with Goat Cheese,
        263–64
    Salmon in Chile Broth, 238–39
    Turkey Cutlets with Roasted Peppers and
        Pepper Jack Cheese, 232

Perfect Roast Chicken, 211

pesticides, 21, 22

Pesto, 212, 214

Pesto-Roasted Chicken, 212–14

pistachios, Butternut Squash with Spinach
        and Pistachios, 151–52

# ABOUT THE AUTHOR

DAVID PERLMUTTER, MD, is a board-certified neurologist and Fellow of the American College of Nutrition who received his MD degree from the University of Miami School of Medicine, where he was awarded the Leonard G. Rowntree Research Award. He is president of the Perlmutter Health Center in Naples, Florida, and the cofounder and president of the Perlmutter Brain Foundation. Dr. Perlmutter serves as a volunteer associate professor at the University of Miami School of Medicine. He is a frequent lecturer at symposia sponsored by such medical institutions as Columbia University, the University of Arizona, Scripps Institute, New York University, and Harvard University. Dr. Perlmutter has been interviewed on many nationally syndicated radio and television programs and networks, including *20/20*, *Larry King Live*, CNN, Fox News, *Fox & Friends*, *The Today Show*, *Oprah*, *The CBS Early Show*, and *The Dr. Oz Show*, where he serves as medical adviser. In 2002 Dr. Perlmutter was the recipient of the Linus Pauling Award for his innovative approaches to neurological disorders and in addition was awarded the Denham Harman Award for his pioneering work in the application of free radical science to clinical medicine. He is the recipient of the 2006 National Nutritional Foods Association Clinician of the Year Award as well as the 2010 Humanitarian of the Year Award from the American College of Nutrition. He has contributed extensively to the world medical literature, with publications appearing in *The Journal of Neurosurgery*, *The Southern Medical Journal*, *Journal of Applied Nutrition*, and *Archives of Neurology*. He is the author of seven books, including the #1 *New York Times* bestseller *Grain Brain*. Dr. Perlmutter serves as editor in chief of the peer-reviewed scientific journal *Brain and Gut*.